Beginning
Philosophy

Beginning Philosophy

Peter Mullen

Edward Arnold

© Peter Mullen 1977

First published 1977
by Edward Arnold (Publishers) Ltd
25 Hill Street, London W1X 8LL

ISBN: 0 7131 0129 6

All Rights Reserved. No part of this publication may be reproduced, stored in a retrieval system, or transmitted in any form or by any means, electronic, mechanical, photocopying or otherwise, without the prior permission of Edward Arnold (Publishers) Ltd.

Filmset in 10/11 pt Plantin and printed in Malta by Interprint (Malta) Ltd

Contents

Preface	v
1 Words Philosophers Use	1
True	1
Knowledge	3
2 Looking at the World—Is There Anything There?	5
Sense Data	6
More Sense Data or What's the Difference?	8
3 The Problem of Meaning—Part One	10
Words and Objects. Words and Ideas.	10
4 Persuasive Definition—Our Vested Interest in the Use of Certain Words	13
The Meaning of Real	14
Words and Feelings—Emotive Meaning	15
5 Fallacies and the Appeal to Authority	17
Science as an Authority	18
The Scope of Science	19
6 The Problem of Existence—How Things Are	21
7 The Problem of Meaning—Part Two	24
Grammar and Sense	24
Missing the Point	24
Ungrammatical Sense?	25
Vagueness	26
Systematic Vagueness	27
8 Personal Identity—Bodies, Minds and Brains	29
9 Evaluative Words—'Good'	33
All Good Things	33
A Satisfactory Compromise?	34
Let's Try to Agree	35
10 Moral Philosophy	36
Morals and Authority	36
Utilitarianism	36
White Lies	39
11 Aesthetics—A Question of Taste?	41
The Critics at Work	41

	Avant Garde Critics	43
	The Critics' Authority	44
	Is Criticism Professional Snobbery?	45
	The Pop Establishment	45
	Summary	46
12	The Problem of Meaning—Part Three	47
	Fallacies	47
	Some not All	47
	In a Circle	47
	Time and Cause	48
13	Causation	49
	Final Cause?	51
14	Definition	53
	Ostensive Definition (1)—Pointing and Talking	53
	Ostensive Definition (2)—Defining the Invisible	54
	Synthetic Definition	55
15	The Existence of God	57
	A Recurring Question	57
	History of the Idea of God—One Approach	57
	God as Creator of Everything?	59
	The Argument from Design	60
	The Problem of Evil	61
	The Argument based on Religious Experience	63
	Summary	64
16	Further Reading	68

Preface

This is not meant to be a systematic course in philosophy. It is an attempt to present in straightforward language some of the problems with which philosophers deal. I believe that when grappling with these problems a peculiar kind of thinking is required. Anyone who has studied philosophy will, I think, know instantly what I mean by that.

The sort of thinking I refer to is one which goes to the edge of total scepticism, which is prepared to entertain what might appear to be outlandish hypotheses and questions. For instance, 'Is the world really as we see it?'. 'Are some actions right and others wrong, or is it just a matter of opinion?'. 'Why does the Universe exist?'. 'Is there a God?'. It may be that, in the end, no one is able to solve these problems. But success here seems to me to be of lesser importance than that people try, for in the struggle with wide and open-ended questions our minds are exercised rigorously and our conceptual horizons widened beyond measure.

It seems to me that no particular school subject heading deals particularly in what we might loosely call 'philosophical thinking'. This is not intended to be a sweeping criticism of the curriculum. I am aware of the difficulties with which teachers are already faced in preparing students for the various subject examinations. In my own subject I have discovered that frequently the main problem is, 'How can I cover this vast syllabus in such a short time?' and only very rarely 'What shall we do when we have finished?'. But in those lessons after the examinations have been endured and completed, I have tried out so called 'philosophical questions' with students of average ability in the secondary school where I work. I was astonished by the result. The questions and puzzles which have been the subject matter of academic philosophy for centuries were of immediate fascination to the students. Of course, no one used the official jargon exemplified by such phrases as 'descriptive metaphysics', 'epistemological criteria' or 'dysteleological surd'. The problems were discussed with great animation and interest and in the language students are used to.

It was an added bonus to find that students carried over the philosophical attitude and method into our regular subject lessons. Many sharp criticisms and more perceptive enquiries from them began to enrich my normal timetable. It is a mistake to leave philosophical thinking to the further education years, as I think the following true story helps to show.

When I was at University I enrolled as an undergraduate philosophy student, as did about thirty-eight others in my year. The first part of the course was fairly straightforward. The tutor dealt with the more obvious fallacies and logical mistakes in his attempt to get us to think properly. This was a great shock to many of us even though, or perhaps *because*, we had passed the rigorous examinations required for university entrance. It was no joke, when just beginning to enjoy your first year of out of school education, to be told that you couldn't think straight! At the end of the introductory year only twelve out of an original forty-two registered to complete the course. When I enquired as to why so many had decided to drop out, I was told by the students themselves that they had not thought philosophy was at all concerned with logic and reasoning but with the collection of happy maxims of the 'Confucius he say . . .' variety. Many undergraduates resented having their essays criticized for this kind of reasoning:

Thomas Aquinas offers proofs for the existence of God.

But these proofs are not valid.

Therefore God does not exist.

I am not wishing to claim that I found philosophy a pushover—far from it! Only that some of us were unprepared for this kind of logical or systematic reasoning even though we had all satisfied what are regarded nationally as high standards for matriculation into the University.

This book has several chapters which deal with the meanings of words and on problems of meaning in general. Some may think that an introduction to philosophy ought to try to steer clear of this area which can be extremely tortuous. From my experience I am bound to say that it was only when my own philosophy teachers introduced the problem of meaning that I began to make any headway in the subject. So I have thought it vital to include some elementary discussion of definition and meaning. At the cost of some oversimplification—which advanced students will spot immediately—I have kept these chapters at the level of a basic introduction.

I am sure that everyone, and particularly students of secondary school age, can successfully be introduced to philosophical method, always provided that this is done fairly informally using straightforward language and omitting most of the academic jargon. This can be of immeasurable interest, lively enjoyment and everlasting benefit to teachers and students alike. I offer this book as something which has grown out of practical experience, hoping that it might help other teachers and students to have as much fun with philosophy as we are having at our school.

Peter Mullen

1 Words Philosophers Use

Philosophy contains a lot of problems. Some might say, 'Philosophy is problems'. The nature of these problems is such that clarity of thought and meaning is essential to their solution. In this respect philosophy resembles arithmetic in the necessity for complete accuracy. For instance, in arithmetic it would be useless to say that 3 + 2 is 'about 5'. When we count we need to know the exact sum of the numbers we are counting, otherwise shopping, wages, pocket money, entrance charges to discos and football games and all the other activities based on counting would collapse.

So it is in philosophy. We need to be clear about the meaning of the words we use. If we are not clear, then our efforts to understand the questions raised by philosophy will become frustrated. Let us begin then with some of the words which we shall frequently come across. We must come to understand them clearly so that we may use them properly.

True

What do we mean when we say that something is true? We use the word in many different situations. That the Olympic Games were held in Montreal in 1976 is true. Men from America landed on the Moon in 1969—true. 3 + 2 = 5, also true. Human beings are either males or females—true. There are lots of situations where we wish to use the word 'true'. But how varied these situations are. 'True' in arithmetic, 'true' in history and personal things which are true about me. Does 'true' have one meaning then or does it have many meanings? Certainly when we use the word in arithmetic it seems to be associated with different things from those with which it is coupled in history or geography. But does this mean that the word 'true' means different things on different occasions? To answer the question we must try to discover what we are doing when we pronounce anything true. We, that is human beings, invented the word 'true' so let us see how we use it. I think we most often use the word to claim that a particular state of affairs is beyond doubt. That is the Olympic Games *were* held in Montreal in 1976. There is no doubt about it. And 3 + 2 *do* make 5, always. There is no room for doubt. There is an atmosphere of completeness and stability of having the last word surrounding any assertion that something is true. Like a checkmate or an ace of trumps, to say something is true is to arrive at a final position—a firm and solid resting place. Look at the final positions the following sentences achieve.

'London is the capital of England, that's quite true.'
'If Tom is younger than Jean then Jean must be older than Tom, that's true.'

'Dickens wrote *David Copperfield*—quite true.'

The words 'that's true' or 'quite true' act as a tick, marking something correct or judging something and finding it accurate. Perhaps we may say, then, at least to begin with, that to say anything is true is to put it in a particular pigeon hole which we might sub-title 'beyond doubt'. This is a very useful pigeon hole; it is a safe spot which acts as the point of departure for further investigation. Once we know that $3 + 2 = 5$, once we say '$3 + 2 = 5$, yes that's true' we can go on to discover the answer to $6 + 4$. When we know it to be true that the Olympic Games were held in Montreal in 1976, we can proceed to ask, 'And which nation won the most medals?' or 'Who finished first in the final of the 10,000 metres at the Montreal Games?'

Of course not all examples are as cut and dried as these. People disagree about what is true and what is not true. But the point is I can only claim that something is not true by claiming that something else is true. I might claim that it is true that the 1976 Olympics were held in Moscow, then we should argue and check with the record books. Eventually we might agree on the truth. Calling something true is isolating that thing and removing other possibilities. To call something true is to reach a point of no compromise. 'The 1976 Olympics were held in Montreal and that is true' means 'The Olympics were not held in Paris or in Moscow or anywhere else; they took place in Montreal.' It does not matter then how strongly someone might argue that these Games were held in another city. That cannot make it true. If you would rather *David Copperfield* had been written by your great grandfather and not by Charles Dickens, once again, sorry but it is true that Dickens wrote the book and that your great grandfather didn't (unless of course you are Dickens' great grandchild!). So in one sense the truth is independent of our wishes and opinions. If something is true, then it is true and no amount of wishing otherwise can alter that. Of course we can work to change states of affairs, but we do not change what is true. For instance it may be true that I am a bad mathematician, but, if I believe my teachers, I can become a good one by working hard instead of lazing over my books. This does not mean that I change the truth into lies. If I ever become a good mathematician then it will be true to say I am a good mathematician; it will remain true that I was once a bad one.

This shows that often truth is related to time and place. I cannot know whether 'It rained' is true or not until some details such as 'in Sheffield last Thursday afternoon' are added. These details are called 'the context'. We may say then that truth needs a context. Notice the different contexts printed in italics in these sentences.

(1) '*In the way we do arithmetic* $4 + 3 = 7$.'
(2) 'There is no atmosphere *on the moon*.'
(3) 'There is no bread left *in our picnic basket*.'
(4) 'Britain was at war with Germany *between 1939 and 1945*.'

If we change the contexts our statements may be true no longer. For instance if we say instead of (4) 'Britain was at war with Germany between 1950 and 1955' then we make a false statement. It is true that Britain was at war with Germany—but not between 1950 and 1955. Therefore we are right to claim that truth often depends upon context. Scientists are careful to be exact about this claim. They do not say 'Water boils at 100°C' but *'Under standard conditions* water boils at 100°C'. In all the examples we have looked at so far, we can see the need for care and accuracy in the use of words. We must be equally careful and accurate when we seek to define, that is give the meanings of words.

Exercise
(1) *Do we always find out whether something is true or not true by looking?*
(2) *Why is it important that everyone should agree that 3 + 2 = 5 is true?*
(3) *Does it make sense to say of anything, 'It's true for me'?*
(4) *Explain the meaning of 'context'.*
(5) *Give an example of a statement which in different contexts may be true or false.*

Knowledge

We use the word 'know' in widely differing ways. We 'know' that London is the capital of England. We 'know' that 3 + 2 = 5. We also 'know' how to read and we 'know' our friends. In these last two cases we usually mean (1) that we possess a certain skill and (2) that we are acquainted with certain people.

When we use 'know' in philosophy we usually mean that we are certain of something. And the word 'knowledge' is reserved for a collection of accurate information. Philosophers rightly insist that we must be absolutely certain of the truth of a statement before we can claim to have knowledge. They insist that we also say *how* we know. We must provide reasons for our claims. So it is not good enough to say 'I know it is 4 o'clock'. If asked we must be prepared to support our claim with something like 'because that wall clock indicates 4 o'clock; it is very reliable and I wound it only ten minutes ago. Besides the radio announcer has just said that it is 4 o'clock'. May we even then claim to know? Most philosophers would probably say we were able to claim knowledge in this case. Some great thinkers, however, have held that there is no knowledge in the world so certain that no reasonable man could doubt it. They have argued that material objects, tables and chairs might be illusions—not really there at all. This may seem silly and completely unreasonable; we shall return to the question later. Sufficient for now to say that it is very hard indeed to *prove* that we know anything at all.

Exercise
(1) *Try to prove that London is the capital of England to a classmate who is perversely arguing against you.*

4   *Beginning Philosophy*

(2) *Do we sometimes use the word 'know' too lightly or without care. If so, why? Give examples.*

We have had a good look at two words which philosophers use, 'Know' and 'True'. There are many others like them, but it would be boring and artificial to deal with them all one by one. Trying to understand two words, as we have tried, is a good way to begin philosophy. We learn how careful we must be in the words we use and perhaps we see some of the possible traps into which careless thinking may lead us. But it is best, in learning a language, to go to the country or area of use so that the language is picked up naturally among native speakers. We should try to pick up philosophy in its natural setting; this means we are best advised to look at the actual problems with which it deals. We shall begin this in the next chapter.

2 Looking at the World—Is There Anything There?

Open your eyes and look around. What do you see? A book? A fire perhaps or a chair? A desk? The windows? Outside, a road, a field, some trees or a cat? Are you sure they are there? How do you know? Surely objects so familiar and solid must be there! Philosophy deals with 'truth' and 'knowledge' and abstract invisible things like that doesn't it? This hard and touchable world in which we live must exist; it must be there in its natural familiarity. In might be quite all right to doubt the existence of ghosts or flying saucers, but it is foolish to deny that there are such things as apples and forks, footballs and record players!

Perhaps it seems odd, but philosophers for thousands of years have questioned the nature of the world as it appears to us. What is it really like? And this last question has encouraged them to ask, 'Is there really anything there at all?'. Ridiculous? Insane? Perhaps. But we can only properly call something ridiculous when we have good reason for our scorn. Is it really so obviously idiotic to believe that the world is not as we see it and even that it may not be there at all?

Let's look at the first question of whether it is idiotic to believe that the world is not as we see it. To put this another way: 'Is the world really just as we see it?'. Imagine school sports day. People are running round a track, others are jumping, still more are seated watching. In the distance there are one or two trees, a few houses and a church tower. Surely I know that there are two trees to the right of the largest house, and the church tower has one window in it! Maybe. But Alice Briggs, who is sitting in a different position, sees the trees to the front of the houses. Moreover, she cannot see the tower at all. Since two people see what we hopefully call the same scene in different ways, how do we know what the scene is really like? Alice has a different picture of the scene; is she right or am I?

Let's leave Alice out of the argument for a minute. Suppose I am alone looking at the same country scene. I call it the same, but it changes. The sun moves round the sky and the window in the church tower suddenly appears to be of dazzling brightness. It wasn't like that five minutes ago. What is the real window like? I put my hand before my eyes to shut out the dazzle. Where is the window now? Behind my hand? How do I know?

We can sum up our argument so far. If the supposed same object appears differently to different people at the same time and to the same person at different times, how can anyone know what the object is really like? We are practical, down to earth beings and we are interested mainly in what the object is 'really' like. How can we find out? To turn now to the second question of whether there is anything really there at all: if we do not know what an object is really like, then it is logically possible that the object is an illusion. In other words it might not be there at all. And if we are uncertain about one object's reality, then we may be uncertain about the reality of any object and in the end of the reality of all objects. So we ask the question which is the title of this chapter. Perhaps this time we ask it believing that it may not be as absurd as we first thought. Is there anything there? Philosophy has made many an attempt to answer this puzzle and has turned up with many different solutions. Let us have a look at some of the more common answers that have been given.

Sense Data

One attempt to answer the question 'Is there anything there?' has been made on the following lines. I see an object differently at different times and from different positions. Therefore what I have is a collection of pictures or information about the object. We call information data; if it comes to our five senses, then it is sense data. From all the pictures we build up out of this data we can intelligently guess, or as philosophers sometimes say, we can 'infer' the existence of something which acts as the source of our data. This something is the physical object, in our case the church tower with its window. The differences of appearance are what we would naturally expect given different perspectives and times from and in which we observe the tower. This answer seems particularly convincing when we can add more evidence in the form of the data which our friends receive and which agrees with ours:
 'Yes the sun does make the window dazzle when it catches the tower at about teatime in June',
 said Alice Briggs.
Many philosophers have asked 'Is there anything there?' and then have been satisfied with the answer just given that we can infer the existence of objects from the sense data which we receive. This solution seems to answer the ordinary demands of our common sense to 'be realistic'.

But there are two objections to this answer many philosophers have thought crucial. First, if I put all the data I have together why should I then think I have a picture of what the object is really like? Why should I imagine that I can infer the nature of the object from this bundle of what we might call 'mental photographs?' It is, after all, always possible that I can add one more photograph to the collection, one which will throw doubt on the authenticity of the others. (e.g. the tower by moonlight). And even if the added, or possible photograph turns out not to be radically different, it is not exactly the same—otherwise it would not count as an additional photograph. Therefore my original collection was incomplete. My actual sense data cannot give a full picture of reality; a picture which is not full is probably inaccurate and therefore inadequate. Besides, if it is objected that an infinite number of sensings of a particular object is not possible within a finite period of time, then how do we know which sensings (or pictures) are necessary to an accurate idea of what the object is actually like? Which data do we keep and which do we discard as irrelevant?

The second objection may be even more telling. 'How can we rely on the collaborated evidence of others when it is not proved that what we call human beings are not our own illusions?' In other words how do I know that the existence of my friend and collaborator Alice Briggs is any more real than the existence of what she is being brought in to evidence? If I can have different data of objects in altered conditions, then I can have different data of people as well. I am in no better position to pronounce on the existence of Alice than I am in to declare the existence of the tower. When this process of doubt is carried on to its logical conclusion the position of 'Only—I—ism' or 'Solipsism' is reached. Solipsism seems to be an absurd position to argue—since it denies what it seems to need to assume, that is the existence of someone to argue with! However, it is sometimes held as a kind of extreme warning to those who argue less than thoroughly. And, absurd as it seems, Solipsism is a suggested answer to the question 'Is there anything there?'. If it is absurd, we ought to be able to show that it is absurd. Although I know of no one who holds Solipsism as a serious philosophical position, it is worth noting that, in his quest for accuracy and certainty, Descartes, the famous French philosopher, seemed to go even beyond it. He suggested at one stage in his programme of systematic doubt that it is possible to doubt the existence of one's own body. However, even Descartes used this extreme form of scepticism only as something on which to build his philosophical system.

Other have suggested that the whole of life is a dream. At first glance this might seem a highly plausible or even an irrefutable hypothesis to a person of sceptical inclination. After all, we sometimes wake from a particularly vivid dream with the strong impression that while we were dreaming we were actually engaged in swimming the Atlantic ocean or chopping trees, as opposed to simply 'imagining these activities in our sleep'.

There are advanced and difficult problems involved here surrounding what we mean by 'sleeping', 'dreaming' and 'waking'. We cannot examine them in detail at this stage. But you might like to consider the view that 'All life is a dream' and see if you can think up any arguments against it.

Exercise
(1) *How do I know that, when I put a stick in water, it does not really bend, but only appears to do so?*
(2) *Is question (1) a sensible question?*
(3) *Is the existence of other people more certain than the existence of objects?*
(4) *Descartes claimed that, in the first place, I have the right to say 'I think therefore I (my mind) am'. Was he right?*
(5) *Are you dreaming now? If so, what are you dreaming about? If not, prove that you are awake.*

More Sense Data or What's the Difference?

Other philosophers accept the power of objections to what we may claim exists, but they say that this is not very important. What does it matter that we cannot discover a reality behind or beyond our sense data? We know, or at least we find, that the world is fairly constant. If we walk on a sense datum of thin ice, it is as if we were walking on thin ice in its result—we fall in. These philosophers are often referred to as phenomenalists because they do not seek any reality behind the data of experience. Phenomena themselves are their own explanation. To ask the question 'What do phenomena represent or point to?' is, for phenomenalism, a pointless question. There is much to be said for this approach. Science functions quite well on it without recourse to physical object questions. After all science deals with the observation and measurement of phenomena. But this solution leaves many students of philosophy with a feeling of unease, it is as if we are shelving an issue or dodging a question. Well, are we? Some philosophers say that the whole procedure of doubt applied to the existence of the world, including the existence of our friends and other human beings, is mistaken from the start. And these philosophers claim that this mistake is based on a misunderstanding of our language. We must look now at this new argument.

When I say, 'I see a church tower' I mean to let you know that there is a church tower and I can see it. 'Church tower' does not mean a collection of sense data, nor does it mean an object compiled or guessed from a collection of sense data. There may be such phenomena as sense data; there is also such an object as the church tower. We do not need to guess the existence of the tower in the same way as we might guess that it is going to rain from the presence of large black clouds. That would be to misuse the work 'guess'. Moreover, it is senseless to complicate the issue by the introduction of an intermediate substance (sense data) between the tower and my eyes. I do not see sense data; I see a tower. This is what I mean when I say 'I see a tower'. If I had wanted to say that I see sense data then I would have said 'I see sense data'. I would not have said 'I see a tower'. When I am in a position to say 'I see a tower' it is nonsense to talk about guessing the existence of the tower. I do not guess or infer it. I see it! Being in a position to see a tower means having my eyes open and nothing impeding my view.

Perhaps you can see that the Phenomenalists and these latter philosophers—let us call them Realists—are in violent disagreement with one another. Each side accuses the other of making an important question trivial and also overcomplicating a simple issue. The Phenomenalist says, 'You are dodging the important question of whether there is anything there or not; besides your reliance on the use of language to support your view is a superficial and irrelevant argument'. The Realist says, 'You are needlessly complicating the issue by the absurd introduction into the argument of such mysterious entities as sense data. And you fail to notice the immense assistance which the way we use language offers to the solution of this problem'.

From here the argument goes on. If you want to examine it more closely then you might find Bertrand Russell's *The Problems of Philosophy* a good help. It contains a short chapter on this subject.

Exercise
(1) *Arrange a debate where one takes the Phenomenalist point of view, and another the view of a Realist.*
(2) *What do you mean when you say 'I see the church tower'?*
(3) *Does it matter whether there are physical objects which give rise to the data we receive?*
(4) *Do you know when your senses are deceiving you?*

3 The Problem of Meaning—Part One

Words and Objects. Words and Ideas

Some people and some books will try to explain to you what words mean. You might think immediately that a dictionary is a good example of this type of book. Of course a dictionary tells us how *people* use words, so what does it mean to say that words have meanings? Sometimes it is said that the meaning of a word is what that word stands for—so 'horse' is a word which stands for an animal with four legs, capable of being ridden etc. In the same way 'school' is a word which stands for a building where people learn about the world. No doubt you can think of many other examples.

There is a difficulty with this idea of what words mean. Not all words seem to stand for objects in the same way that 'horse' and 'school' seem to. For example 'different' is an English word; we all know how to use it, but it is not immediately clear what it stands for. We cannot point to anything and say 'Oh yes, there's a difference over in the corner' as we might well point and say, 'There's a horse and a school'.

This seems to show that words find their meanings in different ways. We might explain the meaning of difference to someone by saying, 'If you take 5 from 12 you will be left with 7. So 7 is the difference between 5 and 12'. We have *pointed out* a meaning quite clearly, but we have not *pointed towards* anything like a horse or a school. It is even more difficult to give the meanings clearly of such words as 'forgetfulness', 'eternity', 'unthinkable' etc. It is to only a very few words which we can point and say 'There is the particular object for which this word stands and that object is the meaning of the word'. Most words are much more difficult to pin down—to *define*. But we use them and understand our use of them so we surely feel we can say that we know what they mean—even if we find it hard to say exactly what they mean when we are asked. Let us look then at another, broader, idea of what is involved in meaning.

There is an argument in the story *Alice Through the Looking Glass* between Alice and Humpty Dumpty about the meaning of words. Humpty Dumpty seems to want to say that words can mean whatever we want them to mean, while Alice is rather doubtful about the possibility of this. We might share Alice's doubt when we think of the likely chaos if part of the population referred to umbrellas as 'puddings'. If we used words to mean whatever we chose them to mean then we should never understand one another, and language, as a form of communication, would break down. So it is necessary that we use our language properly, and that means using words to mean what we all agree they mean.

3 The Problem of Meaning

But there is something in Humpty Dumpty's question 'Who is to be master?' (the words or us). Some people become enslaved to a particular meaning of a word and are subsequently blinded to other meanings of the same word. When this happens to us, our thinking obviously becomes limited, so it is vital that whenever possible we are able to grasp as many variations and shades of meaning as possible. For example, look at the word 'average'. We can use it to mean
(1) half way between a maximum and a minimum score;
(2) the most common score of many different scores;
(3) the total of all the scores divided by the number of scores.

Besides these uses there are other occasions when 'average' is an appropriate word. Sometimes we say that football team's performance was 'only average' and by this we mean to indicate that the team did not play very well. But we also might say of a pupil that his marks were 'up to average' and here we are wanting to let it be known that the pupil has done quite well. Having pointed out five uses of 'average' (and there are others) we can see that an insistence that this word has only one special meaning is to take too narrow a view of the meanings of words. If a father read a report in the newspaper that the play of his favourite football team had been 'only average' he would not be acting in a very fair or reasonable way if he subsequently complained of his son's school report which encouragingly indicated that the boy's work was 'up to the average'.

So we must, when doing philosophy, be absolutely clear and precise in our use of words and neither deliberately nor idly misconstrue the range of their meanings. It is not good enough to call an apple 'a pear'. That is a gross misuse of our language. But it is a mark of ignorance or prejudice to insist that the words 'fair', 'average' and 'reasonable' do not have subtle shades of meaning. In short, within fairly clear rules of language and communication, it is not *words* which mean, but *people* who mean in their usage of words. I think it is no accident that we have in our language such constructions as '*We* mean', '*You* mean' and '*I* mean' as well as '*it* (a word) means'. In the sense which comes most naturally to us it is we, the people, who do the meaning by the context in which we place a word, the mood in which we express it and the situation which we address. Words do not mean anything we wish to mean; Humpty Dumpty held his feelings of power over them inappropriately. But words can be used to mean many things. We are not at their mercy. They are our tools.

Exercise
(1) *Use the word 'reasonable' to*:
   (a) *make a comment about the weather*;
   (b) *ask someone to consider a problem*;
   (c) *make a prediction about a total eclipse.*
   Use good sentences in order to bring out your meaning clearly.

(2) Give examples of three words which can be used in different senses.
(3) Comment on this argument:
 '*John is 16 stones in weight, so he is fat.
 Michael is only $14\frac{1}{2}$ stones, so I would not call him fat*'.
(4) Describe the same situation in two different ways, first making it seem happy and then making it appear unfortunate.
(5) How would you explain the meanings of:
  (a) '*Stop!*';
  (b) '*taller than*';
  (c) '*beautiful*';
  (d) '*tomato*';
  (e) '*Oh bother!*'.

4 Persuasive Definition—Our Vested Interest in the Use of Certain Words

In the last section we saw how the use of words is a subtle and complicated exercise because the meanings of words are not entirely fixed but quite variable. Many people, for instance, parents, friends, governments, teachers, shopkeepers, and yourself use words to encourage or persuade us to do what they think is good for us, or what they would prefer other people to do. Everyone does this, so it is nothing extraordinary or particularly wicked when we find that we do it ourselves, often.

When we say that words can have various meanings, we are saying that they can be *defined* in different ways. When someone uses an argument to persuade us to accept his or her recommended action then we can say that *persuasive definition* is being used. For example, we might like to buy a gramophone record but not have the money, and conversation could go like this:

BOY: 'Can I have this record, dad; it's only 89p?'
DAD: 'That's a lot of money! It's more than a week's spending money.'
BOY: 'But it's less than the cost of the record we bought my sister; that one was £1.05.'
DAD: 'Yes, but it's still more than our tickets for the Wanderers' game.'

Notice that the amount in question, 89p doesn't change. What alters is the way of describing it. The young boy is anxious to make 89p seem only a little, while his father is equally keen to show that it's much more than some other items and therefore a lot of money. In other words the boy is *persuasively defining* 89p as a little; Dad is persuasively defining it as a lot. Each is hoping to change the mind of the other. So we see that persuasive definition is used to get people to accept our own opinions and fall in with our requests. There are many examples of this procedure.

Think of the following:

(1) Signs in shops claiming that certain items are 'only' so many pounds. (What is the value of 'only' here?) If you have a lot of money and are not particularly worried about what you spend it on 'only' might seem a very little. But if you are poor and hungry and you see an electric toothbrush marked 'only' such and such, then 'only' might seem a cruel joke. In fact, 'only' tells us nothing; it merely seeks to persuade us to buy the toothbrush by attempting, illogically, to suggest that the price is not high. Whether the price is high or not for me depends, of course, on how much money I have.

(2) 'United play football as it should be played'.

This is not a piece of information to the effect that United play according to the rules. Presumably all the teams do this or they would be dismissed from the league. No. The writer is trying to persuade us that United are a very good team, not because they have scored more goals than any other, or won more matches (though of course they may have done this as well) but because they 'play football as it should be played'—in other words in the fashion of which the writer approves! Do you see? The writer, perhaps the manager of that football team, is doing nothing else except trying to convince us that his idea of how the game should be played ought to be everyone's idea of excellence. Once again no appeal to any undisputed fact is made. Everything depends on your point of view. If you like United's kind of football, well and good; if you do not like the style then 'as it should be played' uttered by the team's manager should not, on its own, persuade you of the superiority of his team. The sports pages of our papers are filled with this kind of persuasive sentence. We find these examples not only on sports pages. At some time or other almost all of us use persuasive definitions. We have seen how it enters into pocket money bargaining and sales in the high street. Often politicians and clergymen in electioneering and sermons seek to change our attitudes or gain our approval by appealing to words which they think will strike us as above criticism. Some of these are 'honest' 'democracy', 'patriotic', 'moderate' etc, etc. I'm sure you can think of many more.

When politicians and others use these words, they hope to persuade us that no one could possibly take exception to their usage. They suggest, in their clever speeches, that the meaning which they put upon any of these words is the 'real' meaning, and therefore they suggest that it is the only meaning. It is but a short step from there to securing our total acceptance of the views which they wish to convey. The trick is to gain our support for the view by convincing us that there is no other acceptable meaning to the words on which they base their arguments. If this trick succeeds, we are left with no choice but to accept the politicians' or the persuaders' conclusions. If we accept their original definitions of certain critical words, we can deny their conclusions only on pain of contradicting ourselves. The point at which to enter the argument is not halfway through, but at the beginning where the definitions and meanings are being given out. All kinds of bizarre conclusions can follow once we grant the plausibility of original definitions and premises, for example:

(1) 'All schoolboys are small'.
(2) 'John Smith, the schoolboy, is 6 feet 4 inches'.
(3) '∴ John Smith is small'.

Once we have been tricked into accepting (1) as a sensible statement, we are bound to acknowledge the sense of any nonsense which might follow! The antidote is, of course, to avoid accepting nonsensical definitions and contradictory terms.

The Meaning of 'Real'

I don't mean to suggest that all politicians are rogues; it just so happens that they, of all men, are the most famous users of persuasive definitions.

4 Persuasive Definition

Some believe that their cause is so important for the rest of us that it doesn't matter if their methods of convincing us of its necessity for our well being involves some logical sleight of hand—some use of rather strange definitions. Thus political speeches are well worth looking at for an introduction to a critical measure of definitions in argument.

Some words, more than all others, appear to be ready made for logical conjuring tricks. Perhaps the best example of one of these is the word 'real'. Look at the following sentences:

(1) Real tigers have teeth.
(2) Real sailors are not seasick.
(3) If it's a real watch, it will tick.
(4) Any man of real honesty would agree that charity begins at home.
(5) I knew it was a real fish when I saw its fins.
(6) In a real school, games would always be on Friday afternoons.

Perhaps we should like to say that in sentences (1) (3) and (5) 'real' has a genuine, informative function. But in sentences (2) (4) and (6) it functions only as a kind of psychological lever to persuade us to accept the views of the speaker. Psychology has a large part in this kind of persuasion. In (2) we are meant to feel ashamed of ourselves if we are seasick—especially if we want to encourage our friends to believe that we are quite good at sailing! In fact, many sailors are seasick every voyage; they are none the less 'real' sailors for that. Beware of thinking that whenever 'real' appears it is telling us a fact—something true about the world. Often it is a sentence which does convey a fact; but equally frequently it occurs in a statement which is one long piece of persuasion. There are other words like 'real'; perhaps you can think of some yourself. Good examples include 'true,' 'average' and 'honest' as well as such phrases as 'plain to see' or 'it is obvious'. These last two are most frequently introduced when the conclusion which the propagandist wants us to accept is very far from 'plain to see' or 'obvious'. In the same way the much used word 'surely' never lends any real weight to an argument—so far as the logic of the argument is concerned. It remains a very powerful persuader.

Words and Feelings—Emotive Meaning

One of the most subtle and effective methods of persuasion by the use of words plays upon our emotions, or feelings. The first step is to get us to accept that a group of people, an idea or a belief is distasteful or undesirable. The next step is to use the word which names or describes that group as if it meant 'bad'. Finally, if we do not exercise the utmost care in our thinking, we can be led to believe that any bearer of that name or description, or even anyone or anything remotely associated with it, is bad. This happens with words like 'foreigner', 'communist', 'capitalist' and 'black'. For example look at the sentence, 'We must root out this wicked capitalist plot'. Now notice we are not told whether the plot is wicked because it is capitalist or capitalist because it is wicked. (There may of course be entirely

different considerations at work.) But the general aim of persuasive sentences of this type is to get us to think that either
(1) some plot is bound to be wicked because it is a capitalist plot, or
(2) the plot in question is particularly wicked because it is a capitalist plot.

The final aim of all such devices is to persuade us that some words which are not originally moral in meaning do in fact carry such a meaning or force. So some people always feel themselves to be getting angry when they hear the word 'imperialist', 'socialist' or 'negro'. Thinking people ought not to be misled by such arguments which make an emotional rather than a logical and rational appeal.

To end this section let us look at some words which have both a descriptive and an emotive (a feelings aroused) meaning. 'Lazy' is perhaps a good example. Maybe a lazy person could make out a good case for the lazy existence—lack of tension, more carefree, less liable to stress diseases, therefore happier etc, etc. But when a propagandist uses 'lazy' he usually means to show his disapproval (and also gain our disapproval, of course!) of the person whom he correctly describes as 'lazy'. See if you can think of your own examples; here are a few more: 'atheistic', 'religious', 'adolescent' and 'odd'. Remember, in the world of definition, meaning, argument and persuasion a cool, calm approach is needed together with a determination not to be taken for a ride.

Exercise
(1) *Is 'only' a dangerous word?*
(2) *Is there such a thing as an honest argument?*
(3) *Write a report of a game of football and then underline the parts of the report which are not informative but persuasive.*
(4) *Show how the word 'good' can be used to persuade someone that he ought to accept your opinions.*
(5) *Make a list of as many emotive (feeling aroused) words as you can. How many of them have ordinary, descriptive meanings as well?*

5 Fallacies and the Appeal to Authority

We have looked at one or two ways by which others seek our agreement through the use of persuasive definitions. There are many other faults in arguments commonly used and it is important that we notice when they occur. For example:
(1) The proofs of God's existence are by Thomas Aquinas;
(2) but these proofs are not convincing;
(3) ∴ God does not exist.

This is a typical mistake or fallacy. (3) does not follow from (1) and (2) because even if St Thomas Aquinas is mistaken it may still be true that God exists. It is simply that Aquinas has got his proofs wrong. Someone else may have other, more convincing proofs; but even if no such proofs exist this has no bearing on whether there is a God or not. The existence of any object is obviously quite distinct from the arguments in favour of that object's existence. The fact that Aquinas is wrong about proofs cannot be used as an argument for the non-existence of God. We would do rightly if we substituted for (3) '∴ They are not proper proofs.'

Not every example of this kind of logical mistake is so easy to detect. Sometimes the fallacy is concealed by a great many words. But once you have seen the form of the fallacy, you should be on your guard against future examples.

Another method widely used to gain our agreement is the appeal to authority. Arguments of this kind suggest that:
(1) 'Everyone knows...'
(2) 'All the best people can...'
(3) 'The Professor himself believes...'
(4) 'The Bible says...'

These ought similarly to persuade us of nothing. Usually when someone argues 'Everyone knows...' he means 'You ought to think or believe...', while 'All the best people' is simply a form of blackmail, an attempt to make you feel a lesser being if you do not agree with the speaker. As for 'The Professor himself believes', what on earth is the relevance of the fact that the Professor believes something? No doubt another professor can be found who disagrees with *the* Professor! Who is then to say which professor is correct?

Religious people frequently appeal to the Bible. But the statement 'The Bible says' has no power, or at least ought to have no power, to convince unless we are *already* believers in its infallibility. There is no reason why a Hindu or a Moslem should regard 'The Bible says...' as any argument for believing or doing a particular thing or act. These people have their own religious books. There is no reason why they should accept the tenets of the Christians as prescriptions for action. The appeal to the Bible can only, logically, persuade when we have accepted or are prepared to accept its authority on other grounds. If we become Christians and believers in the Bible then the preacher has a right to direct our minds to the instructions and doctrines found within it. But if we do not accept the Biblical religion then all appeals to the Bible are empty, having no logical power to persuade. In short, all appeals to any kind of authority only have force when that authority has been accepted by the person who is being persuaded.

Science as an Authority

There is no general immunity against this way of being deceived. Scientists, in their worse moments, often use a similar form of argument. Usually this variation begins: 'It is physically impossible . . . ' or 'It has been chemically proved that . . .' which sometimes act as barriers to our further questionings. Suppose you find an iron bar and heat it, discovering that it expands with the heat, then a physicist may tell you that it has stretched in accordance with a physical law that metal expands when it is warmed in flame or by the sun. This is quite acceptable in the majority of cases. But one day someone might find an iron bar, heat it, and discover it does not expand. One of two consequences follows: either it was not an iron bar in the first place; or the formula about expanding metals must be revised in order to cope with the new situation. Be sure that physicists, who are after all, as conservative as all other people, will resist all pressure to alter their law about iron bars. But if the substance found really is iron, then the formula or law will have to be changed. This is the way that progress is made in science. Protectors of the old theory or the old law may argue that 'It is physically impossible that an iron bar should not expand when heated'. But these protests will ultimately fail because you have, actually in your possession, an iron bar which will not expand when heated.

The temptation to slowness on the part of scientists to admit exceptions to their theories is understandable. The laws with which they explain to us the working of the world have been drawn up often, only after hours and even years of painful research and discovery. No one is particularly willing to see all his work overuled by an exception, such as an iron bar which will not expand when heated. But we must remember that the laws of the scientists about the world are not necessarily true for ever. They are statements which help up to recognize a regular sequence of events; they warn us what to *expect*. So a fair way of expressing the rule or law 'Metal expands when heated' is 'When you heat a piece of metal, *expect* it to expand'. There is one very good reason why the scientists' rules cannot be shown to be true for ever and that is simply because tomorrow is not here yet! Tomorrow someone might find a substance which is like a metal in every other respect except that it will not expand when heated. It is unreasonable to expect scientists or anyone else to tell us exactly what will happen tomorrow; but science does give us good general rules about what to expect from the world we live in. Beware, though, of expecting too much from science; it can tell us only what is most likely to happen, not exactly what will happen. Just as we should beware of the preacher, the politician or the salesman who makes large claims for his version of the truth, so we must be careful to avoid being misled by what are often called 'scientific laws' or 'physical facts'.

The Scope of Science

Just because the statements of science are not always true forever does not make them worthless. A famous philosopher, Bertrand Russell, used to argue that the scientist has no proof that the sun will rise tomorrow. All the occasions when the sun has risen in the past, he ways, are not evidence that it will rise tomorrow. This argument used to carry a lot of weight, but its influence was due more to the respect with which people treated anything said by Lord Russell than to any rational appeal of the argument itself. Lord Russell seems to use the words 'proof' and 'evidence' in a very restricted and narrow way. Of course, as we have already noted in the case of the iron bar, we cannot say exactly what is going to happen in the future—simply because the future is not yet with us for us to prove our predictions. But we have good evidence amounting almost to proof that the sun will rise tomorrow; we have every reason to think that it will rise. 'What', we might ask, 'does Lord Russell *expect* the sun to do?'. Once again we are back to the idea that science teaches us what we can expect generally to occur. No doubt there will be exceptions, but, on the whole, the rules which science gives us about the world are reliable and therefore we ought to respect natural science, be grateful for the regularities which it teaches, and learn not to expect the impossible from a study which teaches us about probable occurrences.

Exercise

(1) *If Professor White says, 'x is the case' and Professor Black replies, 'You're wrong; y is the case' whom should we believe?*
(2) *Do people have an uncritical view of the authority of the Bible or of science? If so, why do you think this is the case?*
(3) *Imagine you are called upon to give a lecture entitled 'The Use of Science'. Write a talk on the scope and benefits of scientific methods.*
(4) *Give the talk referred to in question 3 and let it be the basis for an informal discussion.*
(5) *Invent an implausible, because invalid, argument like the one, above, on Thomas Aquinas and God. Say why it is invalid.*
(6) *What kinds of phrases will do as well as 'All the best people' and 'The Professor himself' in arguments which appeal to authority?*

(7) *If you find an iron bar which does not expand when you heat it*:
   (a) *is it an iron bar? or*
   (b) *does it contradict a scientific law?*
(8) *What's wrong with 'The Bible says' as an incentive to believe the truth of a statement?*

6 The Problem of Existence— How Things Are

What do we mean when we say that something exists? We use the word frequently of all kinds of things. Trees exist, I exist, colours exist, music exists, stories exist, fears exist etc, etc. You might think there is no problem here; isn't it obvious what we mean when we claim that something exists? Unfortunately, no; it isn't always obvious.

To begin with it looks as if different items in our list exist in different ways—the existence of a colour does not seem to be the same kind of thing as the existence of a sound. And the being of a post office is not like the being of a picture in my imagination. These differences have encouraged philosophers and others to talk as if one kind or mode of being is *real* while the other modes are somehow less real. So you might hear it said that a door is real (or exists) while a prediction, a memory or a calculation is 'only an idea'. But it must be true that all names of objects point to something which exists in one mode or another, or they would not be useful as names. Simply because one class of objects can be seen and touched does not by itself provide sufficient reason for us to suppose that that class of objects is more real than a class of objects which, for instance, exists when we use imagination. Ask yourself, 'Is a toothache as real as a barn door?' I think you will agree that it is at least as real! Especially so while you are suffering that ache! But in the tranquillity of a philosophical discussion, away from all discomfort, it seems strange to say that pains are as real as barn doors.

Perhaps the root of the confusion is once again centred on the use of words. The word 'real' is sometimes taken to mean 'solid' or 'touchable'. Now it is obvious that some things are more easily touchable, more solid than others—barn doors than pains, for instance. But it is a mistake to suggest that therefore barn doors are more real than pains. But this is the mistake most easily made in all conversations about existence; the temptation to make one thing out to be *more real* than another. Perhaps we ought to say that there is no one thing any more real than any other; all things which have names exist in one of a variety of different ways. Just because certain modes of existence, or at least the objects which exist in these same modes, are more useful to us, it does not follow that all other named objects which do not exist in these same modes do not exist at all.

There are difficulties and temptations even with this view. Some have suggested that if we admit the existence of, say, unicorns (in the mode of the imagination or the mode of fairy tales) then we are on a slippery slope leading us to the absurdity of admitting the existence of round squares and white black squares. But in fact we are on no slippery slope because we can, after all, say what we mean by the existence of a unicorn—'A unicorn is something which you will not meet in the street, but might well read about in a book of fairy tales'. Even the contradictory idea of the round square might reasonably, or at least facetiously, be said to exist in the world of philosophical examples! We must avoid the mistaken assumption that to say something exists is to suggest that we can shake hands with it, open it, drink it or otherwise touch it. It does make sense to say all the following:

(1) 'Snails exist in my back garden'.
(2) 'Hamlet exists in Shakespeare's play'.
(3) 'The Minotaur exists in Greek Mythology'.
(4) 'The multiplication sign exists in mathematical language'.

Notice that in all these cases we qualify, or say what we mean by 'exists' when we use the phrases beginning 'in . . . '. Of course, it would be a mistake to ascribe certain abilities and functions to some of these objects other than the roles which the names of them play in the sentences where they are used. For example, it is accurate to state that Minotaurs exist in Greek Mythology; but it would be absurd to go on and suggest that we had all better look out or we might be butted by one of them! It is always the context which allows us to claim that something exists. We are allowed to say that a thing *is* when we can say *where* it is. This is true even, in a silly sense, when we don't know where it is—when it is lost. For even when we don't know where it is, when it is lost, we know what it would be like for it not to be lost. Think of anything and it exists, even if only in your imagination.

As we hinted in the case of the Minotaur there is a need for us to say what we mean when we refer to the modes of existence. The names of all existing objects fall into many different classes or categories. The philosopher who wants to deny the existence of certain kinds of objects is only cautiously and for our own good advising us against confusing the categories—e.g. of 'imagination' and 'material objects'. If he is not merely doing this, but wanting to deny completely the existence of classes of named objects, then the cautious philosopher is perhaps being too scrupulous, revising away our concepts so that what remains fits more neatly into his scheme of things.

To show more clearly what is meant here it is useful to make a statement which at once can be provocative and uncontroversial. For instance, 'I believe in ghosts'. If I mean by this to convey that I think there are such things as departed spirits which can appear in this world, then I am open to correction. It is perfectly possible to argue against this view quite rationally. But if I say that what I really mean by 'I believe in ghosts' is that I think that in 'Hamlet' and in 'The Turn of the Screw' there are ghosts about which we may read, then I am not making any kind of controversial statement. In other words, if I want to suggest that there are such objects as ghosts, the spirits of the dead, which shock and scare us when they appear, then you are perfectly free to disagree with me. You may say clearly, 'There are no ghosts', and argue the case very persuasively. But if I merely state that there are ghosts in certain plays and novels by Shakespeare and Henry James, then you can hardly take exception to my utterance. It is important to indicate or make plain the context in which you are speaking (everyday life or novels for example) because that is the context in which you will then be understood.

The same kinds of arguments hold good with such statements as 'God exists', 'Ice creams exist' or 'The weather forecast exists'. There is no level on which we can say absolutely that something does not exist. Those things to which names refer have being somewhere, even if only in the imagination. There is the different question, of course, of whether there are ghosts which are departed spirits, whether there is a God who made us, or even whether there is a piano in my sitting room. The important thing is to realize that this is a different question, another issue.

Exercise
(1) *What is similar about a violin and an orange, and how do they differ?*
(2) *How would I discover that the following have being:*
 (a) *apples?* (c) *philosophers?*
 (b) *vampires?* (d) *question marks?*
(3) *How is it possible to claim that ghosts exist without also claiming that they are spirits of the dead?*

7 The Problem of Meaning—Part Two

Grammar and Sense

You must have noticed, by now, how language can confuse. There is hardly anything straightforward about it. Let us look at some of the ways in which language is often misused, and sometimes deliberately employed, in a misleading way. Language not working properly should be called 'nonsense' or 'rubbish'.

Missing the Point

Can a sensible sentence ever be rubbish? I think we might want to say 'No' to that. Surely a sensible, straightforward and grammatical sentence can't be rubbish. Don't we all understand 'It is a paper aeroplane' and 'There are no seals in Windermere'? It would be difficult to imagine occasions when these sentences could be meaningless—and yet such occasions do exist.

Suppose someone asks, 'What is the capital of England?' and someone else replies, 'It is a paper aeroplane'. There is an obvious example where we would want to say that 'It is a paper aeroplane' had no meaning. But the *reason* it has no meaning is the most interesting part. It has no meaning not because we can't tell what the words mean, but because in the context of a reply to the question 'What is the capital of England?' the words 'It is a paper aeroplane' are meaningless. Now we all understand the meaning of 'It is a paper aeroplane' but we cannot understand these same words as an answer to 'What is the capital of England?' So we see that whether or not a sentence has any meaning depends not only on its being grammatically correct and consisting of real words, but also on the *context* in which it is used. As an answer to the question, 'What is that you are throwing across the classroom?' the statement 'It is a paper aeroplane' makes complete sense. But in another context it makes no sense at all. It is literally nonsense—rubbish.

Not all examples of rubbish are so easily spotted as this one. Sometimes the sentence, phrase or answer which is rubbish appears to be completely sensible. We have already seen how politicians and preachers are good at using words in persuasive ways. One of the most persuasive ways of talking is that which makes use of an apparently reasonable sentence to make a completely irrelevant comment, statement or reply. So politicians sometimes talk sense. But if that sense is not about the question at issue, then it might as well be nonsense or rubbish.

For example, suppose a politician is asked a direct question—one which embarrasses him and his party, how does he deal with it without appearing

7 The Problem of Meaning

to be a fool or a rogue? Experienced politicians usually dodge this kind of question by talking 'beside the point'.

QUESTION: 'Why didn't your party build more houses in Wales when you were last in power?'
ANSWER: 'When we were last in power we built more houses in the South of England than were ever built by the other party.'

We are tempted to say, 'Very good. We're glad you built a lot of houses somewhere, but you were asked specifically about houses in Wales'. This kind of reply, talking beside the point, and not at or on the point at issue is a kind of nonsense or rubbish simply because it is not relevant. It is no use in this particular context. It is like the reply 'It's a paper aeroplane' to the question, 'What is the capital of England?' So beware! Even when a sentence looks or sounds perfectly sensible, it may not be. Examine the situation in which it is spoken. Is it relevant? Is it on the point at issue? Is it in context? If it is not, then despite its apparent sense it is beside the point —rubbish.

Ungrammatical Sense?

We have seen how it is quite easy to talk grammatically and yet fail to make sense. Is it possible to misuse the English language and still communicate? In other words, is it true that we sometimes speak incorrectly, as far as the rules for using our language are concerned, but we manage to get what we mean across?

It is obvious that, if we are to share a language, then we must agree on the meanings of words in that language. It would be no good if you meant by 'tree' what I mean by 'rabbit'. Catastrophe would result if some used 'safe' where others used 'dangerous'. So we must have rules about using words in a consistent way. But how strictly ought these rules to be enforced? What standard of correctness should we aim for? Clearly the extreme contradictions in the examples about 'tree' and 'rabbit', 'dangerous' and 'safe' will not be permitted.

But if we look at text books of English Grammar we shall find that many rules for the use of our language are so refined and obscure that most of us get along quite well without ever understanding their relevance. For instance, why should it be said to be correct sometimes to use 'should' and on other occasions 'would'? I think the answer is that we must be able to express ourselves *precisely* in language, and therefore complicated rules which cover all conditions have appeared. But for most of our everyday speech we can get by without attention to the more obscure rules of speech.

The question is 'How far can we go along the way, disregarding the rules of grammar?' The answer to this is not simple. Sometimes it seems we can go a long way, flouting the rules; on other occasions we lose our ability to communicate accurately as soon as we make a simple oversight. For instance we should still be clearly understood if we said 'The man *are* here' instead of the more precise 'The man *is* here'. The same goes for the common mistake of the schoolboy 'We *was* coming' for 'We *were* coming'. Both are examples of a misuse of the rules of language not interfering with the sense of the message which we are trying to convey. This kind of situation occurs frequently, especially in more subtle forms. So in one sense it is possible to speak nonsense and still be understood.

But it is doubtful if we should ever convey a clear meaning by 'As high as a nail' for 'As high as a kite'. The simple misplacing of one word wrecks the whole sentence. This kind of happening is also a common occurrence, but it is easy to point to the reason for it. Usually, it comes about through a lack of understanding of the meaning of a word, a *particular word*. And, of course, I have chosen here an obvious extreme example. But the mistake of the first kind, in which we break a grammatical rule, but where we are still understood, is an error involving the understanding of a *rule*.

From this we can be sure that language is a flexible thing. It can be bent this way and that any yet remain an adequate vehicle for communication. We do understand the faltering attempts at sentence construction made by young children. But it is equally important to remember that there are obvious limits. Once we begin to use words or to apply rules in abnormal or strange ways, the function of language as communication will fail and we shall no longer understand one another.

Vagueness

It's one thing to talk about rules of language and how to obey them; it's quite another thing to learn how to use that language well. We have all met people who seem completely at home with words; people who always have an apt word; people of whom we say, 'He can talk'. We can all talk, of course; and we can all write. It's just that some are better than others at these skills. A mark of good speech is the ability to use words with accuracy, to say exactly what we mean, to convey precisely what we intend to convey and not something else. When we fail to do this, we are not necessarily breaking any grammatical rules, but we are being *vague*. Vagueness is a disadvantage in most of ordinary conversation and it is a cause of mistakes in philosophical argument and reasoning. Here are some words which are vague. Do you use them? 'Big', 'Nice', 'Good', 'Poor' etc. There are occasions when it is perfectly suitable to use them; but mainly they are vague words and do not say anything very clearly about a subject. So people say 'It is a nice day' when 'It is a hot, sunny and close day' would convey much more information and describe the day much more accurately. The same goes for 'A good play' when we might have said 'A tense, enthralling, though sometimes very humorous play'. No doubt you can think up many more examples like these.

It is much better, in almost every area of life, to use the apt word, the precise word, the descriptive word. Whether it be in ordering the Sunday

7 The Problem of Meaning

joint, writing after a job or answering a letter or phone call, the specific word is the one to use. This is especially true when it comes to reasoning and philosophy. If, as part of a philosophical discussion, you are wanting to say 'All generous men enjoy a reward' then you can only make that point forcibly by using the word 'generous' and not some other word. If you say 'good' instead of 'generous' you are not only being less accurate, but might even be said to be inconsistent, since a good man is not necessarily (though of course he may be) generous.

As you know, it is very difficult to argue clearly. It becomes almost impossible to carry on a satisfactory argument when vague words are being used. This is another aspect of language which is greatly exploited by politicians and preachers. They know that words such as 'free' and 'wrong' are capable of being defined in so many different ways—because of their vagueness—that they can be used even by political opponents to make a general appeal. Look at this sentence:

'All free men will join together to oppose and defeat wrong'.

Well, of course, they will! But the point is what do the words 'free' and 'wrong' mean precisely? This sentence could be spoken in all honesty and conscience by a Conservative, a Socialist, an Anarchist, an Atheist, a Liberal—in short, by anyone. Why is this? It is because the words 'free' and 'wrong' are left undefined. They are vague. As soon as the Anarchist says what he means by them he will come into immediate conflict with the Liberal. And this is because each means by them quite different things. For example, the Liberal may assume, or at least suggest, that political subversion is wrong. The Anarchist might believe such subversion to be the appropriate and moral course of action on some occasions. It is only when they 'unpack' or say what they mean by the word 'wrong' that their disagreement becomes apparent. Until this happens the argument is under the universal blanket, or cloud, of vagueness. This is sometimes exactly what the politicians and preachers desire—to appeal to as large an audience as possible by using words which win universal approval but which nonetheless remain vague. For example, it is difficult to imagine anyone wanting to object to a party which pledges itself to policies which are for 'the good of the state'. But let each party say what is meant by 'good' and open disagreement will replace the apparent unity which was supposed to exist before.

Systematic Vagueness

Sometimes it is not a bad thing to allow for vagueness. When we are not clear about the precise meaning of a word, it is good not to try to define it too closely. Or when we meet a new object or event it is sometimes best to delay making an immediate classification. For example, we can give a general name to cover all the objects in each of the following lists:

| Glider | Cruiser | Helicopter | Liner |
| Monoplane | Destroyer | Biplane | Yacht |

The first list of items can be headed 'aircraft' and the second list 'ships'. No doubt you could add many other objects to these lists without making a mistake. But which list would 'hovercraft' belong to? It is difficult to decide. Here is an example of a new invention which in many ways resembles a ship, but because it doesn't float on the water, but flies just above the surface, it is much like an aircraft. Very well, let us not be in a hurry to force the object into one class or the other. An exception to both classes ought not to worry us unduly; our language is flexible enough to cope with new objects and events. The fact that we are able to describe the hovercraft proves this. Eventually classification is necessary if confusion is to be avoided, but it does no harm to wait and see whether any new aids to definition turn up.

At present 'death' is a word which is hard to define or to classify. This is because the traditional idea of death has been altered by innovations such as the heart transplants. At one time it was easy to say that 'death' is a word meaning the state of a body whose heart has stopped beating for more than (say) twenty minutes. But the transplant has enabled doctors to keep a person alive with a different heart in his body. Patients once given up for dead have been revived. Machines which record electrical activity in the brain have indicated the presence of movement and life long after the traditional certificate of death might have been written. The doctors are investigating the possibilities of prolonging life and postponing the finality of death. So it may be many years before a satisfactory definition of 'death' is arrived at. In the meantime, problems remain for doctors and coroners' courts. The word death is 'floating'. It has no precise meaning. But the point is, as in the case of 'hovercraft', it can still meaningfully be used. So we see that while vagueness is generally to be avoided, it is sometimes an advantage to draw the boundary lines of definition less rigidly.

Exercise
(1) *Give examples of sentences which are grammatically incorrect, but which are still meaningful.*
(2) *What does it mean to 'miss the point'?*
(3) *What is wrong, if anything, with this reasoning:*
   (a) *'I know I wasn't outside the room, according to school rules, but neither was anyone else'.*
   (b) *'Crimes of violence have increased since the abolition of the death penalty for murder, therefore the death penalty should be restored'.*
(4) *How do politicians evade difficult questions by talking 'beside the point'? Invent examples.*
(5) *Make the following sentence more clearly descriptive by substituting more exact words in place of vagueness. 'It was a dark night when the big man came over the road carrying the nice parcel in his hands'.*
(6) *Make a list of vague words. Make another list of more precise words which can be put in their places.*
(7) *Is it true that sometimes the vague word is the best one to use?*

8 Personal Identity—Bodies, Minds and Brains

'Well even if I can be certain about very little in the outside world, I do at least know who I am!' But even this is open to doubt and enquiry. Nonsense? Well let us begin with our bodies which we can see and touch. Surely I know what my hand is! I can see it, control it, write with it. I feel pain if I burn it, I am aware of coldness when I pick up snow or ice. There is nothing so obviously and simply 'mine' as the hand which I am now using to guide my pen to form words.

But what does it mean to say that my hand is 'mine'? That it is a part of my body? And what, then, do I mean by *my* body? If we think for a moment it becomes clear that when we use 'my' in the case of 'my pen' or 'my book' we are using the word in quite a different way from the way we use it in 'my body'. I can say that my pen belongs to me, but would it mean anything to say 'my body belongs to me'? In either case what is this 'me' to which I refer? In short 'Who do I think I am?' Who do you think you are?

Perhaps my body is owned by my mind in the same way that I own my pen and my book. But this seems to be a queer thing to say, mainly because my body has an effect on my mind, on my whole person, which the pen never has. Besides I can distinguish clearly between what is my body and what is my pen or book, but I cannot tell so obviously the difference or the relation between my mind and my body. Of course, I control my pen, but do I control my body in the same sort of way? It seems not. Some activities of my body I can control, for example, whether I go for a walk or not, whether I have one lump of sugar in my tea, but other actions cannot be similarly controlled. I mean 'blinking', 'digesting' and 'crying' for instance. So my body is neither owned nor controlled by my mind in any normal sense of the words 'owned' or 'controlled'.

All the time we have been arguing this point, we have assumed that we know what the mind is—for we have spoken with confidence of it owning or not owning, controlling or not controlling the body. But it looks as if it is at least as difficult to talk about the mind as it is to talk about the body. For what is the mind? Where is it located? One answer, often given, is that the mind is the brain. The rise of medical science and of psychology encourages this opinion. Scientists have discovered that certain events in the brain are somehow linked to the actions which our bodies perform. So they have gone on to suggest that all bodily activity has a simultaneous activity in the brain. This includes thinking, dreaming, wishing, counting, talking etc ... and even all the activities which require no obvious movement or speech. Therefore, so it is said, the sentence 'The mind is related to the body' is a less precise version of the sentence 'The brain interacts with the body by means of electrical and chemical processes which can be recorded and measured'. Psychologists have machines for recording this activity in the brain. They note that a machine called an electro-encephalograph, attached electrically to the head, records different signals and wavelengths according to whether the subject is dreaming, in a deep sleep or wide awake. They then argue that what we call mental events are really kinds of physical, chemical and electrical events. Their suggestion is backed up by the reports from doctors and surgeons of changes in the behaviour of patients who have had, as treatment, part of their brains removed.

What do we think of this theory? Does it seem reasonable to conclude that, thanks to the electro-encephalograph and the progress of surgery, we can use the words 'mind' and 'brain' to mean the same object? Well some people are convinced and satisfied by the neatness and scientific plausibility of the account. They reason that, just as medical knowledge has increased in other areas of research, so it has in the study of the brain. And now that we can literally see into someone's head, it is obvious that what was once called 'the mind' is electro-chemical activity in a large organ called 'the brain'. The straightforward appeal of this view is not easy to resist.

Others are not satisfied by this scientific and medical account. One argument against it asks what exactly are the pictures we see when we imagine or dream something? If I picture 'in my mind' my father where is that picture exactly? If we cut open my head will the picture appear? Of course not! But where does this leave the 'mind = brain' hypothesis? It suggests that there are other things in my head apart from nerve cells and electrical current. Where are the pictures and the imaginings which we 'see' so clearly? It seems that we must admit they are somewhere. Even an hallucination exists.

Scientists and psychologists are rarely put off by this objection. They argue that for all practical purposes the mind is the same thing as the brain—in thinking, remembering, dreaming and deciding etc and that the 'pictures' we have referred to are a kind of extra, a bonus, or as they sometimes say technically—epiphenomena. They are not necessary to the proper function of the brain; they are a mere accompaniment to the brain's essential activity. However, this psychologists' reply is not always accepted. Many people, myself among them, want to say that the persistence of events like dreams and imaginings and memories in pictorial imagery are proof that the mind can only partly be described as the brain. There seem to be other powerful though less tangible objects in the mind than nerve cells and electric current. Besides it is strange to say 'I have a picture in my *head*'. Where in my head? I don't know. I only know that an incision will not reveal it.

Even if we leave the mind-brain-body problem and turn aside to ask the more direct question, 'Who or what am I?' It seems we are still on unsure ground. I recognize that there is someone called Peter Mullen, an ongoing creature with a body, memories, plans, expectations and relationships with other people. But when I come to say, 'What is the nature of this being named Peter Mullen?' I am by no means clear. And yet I act as if I am absolutely certain about the answer to this question. I make plans and promises on the assumption that I am in control of my life and consciousness, but that same life and consciousness is notoriously difficult to define.

My body is not the same body it was yesterday. Food and drink have been taken in, dead cells have been replaced and my internal organs have been subtly altered in the process of repair. My mind is full of new experiences, fresh ideas and new thoughts. Even my brain has fewer cells than it had yesterday. So in what sense can I even begin to make the claim that I am the same person today as I was yesterday? Mind, brain and body have been changed and modified.

Perhaps it is relevant to notice that in many cases, so far as the world is concerned, I am whom other people say I am. Look at the following list:
(1) The eldest child of James and Iris Mullen.
(2) The brother of Carol Mullen.
(3) The wing three-quarter for West Leeds Old Boys Rugby Team.
(4) The father of Petra Mullen.
(5) The R.I. teacher at Whitecroft High School.
(6) The driver of the car PUG 434G.
(7) The arranger of the trip to Blackpool.

All these descriptions can and do (or did) refer to me. They are used on different occasions by many people to identify me in their conversation with me and about me. The descriptions do not simply label me; they also prompt me to act in different ways in varying situations. It is as if 'Peter Mullen' stands for many different functions and roles. Or for some creature who plays many different parts or games according to the company he keeps on various occasions. To this extent it is true to say that *Who you are depends upon whom people around you say you are.* The football player is a footballer to the crowd on a Saturday afternoon, but he is husband and father to his wife and children. It is also true to say that we accept the roles and parts accorded us by our neighbours for the most part without question. At school I am happy to be a teacher, at home a father, and in the shop a customer. This is not to say that we have no choice in who we are; just that once having accepted a role, having made a decision to act in a certain way, we are bound to conform to that role and abide by that decision for some limited period of time or chaos would erupt. For instance when I am driving my car I am first of all and importantly a driver. In the bank I am first of all a client. So what I am depends upon what I am doing.

Of course for the greatest part of the time we do not look into ourselves and ask profound questions such as, 'Who am I'? Normally we are, in a real sense, what we are doing. But when we do stop and think about our personal identity we are met with large and difficult problems, for we have seen that in mind, body and brain we are changed every day.

It is perhaps possible to find the key to what we are by asking questions which involve us in talking about purpose. For purpose is concerned with thinking, planning and willing. The fact that we continually build on the past to shape our future suggests at least that if we do not know exactly what we are, we do have a deep sense of ongoing unity of intention and purpose. And, aside from this, it may be quite the wrong kind of question to ask about the essential nature of any human being.

Exercise
(1) 'The mind is to the body like a pilot to a ship'—discuss this.
(2) What changes in our body affect our mental states?
(3) Where is last night's dream?
(4) What is memory?
(5) If we change in many ways each day, how can we claim to be the same person?

9 Evaluative Words—'Good'

One thing is certain, if you try to say what 'good' means you will find many people who will reject your definition. How does this disagreement come about? Surely 'good' is not such a hard word that there should be too much argument about its meaning! The best way to solve the problem is to try and give a few examples of possible meanings. Let's suppose for the time being that 'good' is the name of something that belongs to objects in the way that colours or tastes seem to belong to objects. This is to say that 'good' is the name of a quality like hardness or sweetness.

If we want to suggest that 'good' names a quality, we are bound to admit immediately that it is a very strange quality since there is no straightforward way of knowing whether the quality is present in any particular object or not. Most people would agree on the presence of hardness or sweetness in an object, and there are accepted procedures for testing for these qualities. Even, speaking quite loosely, we feel we know what hardness is. An object is hard if it resists the pressure of an open palm, if it hurts in a blunt sort of way when we fall on it etc. But what is it in an object which makes us want to call that object 'good'? If 'good' does name a quality, it is clear that that quality is not evident to our normal senses. I mean, you cannot 'see', in the way we see with our eyes, that something is good. Goodness cannot be heard or felt; the ears and fingers are useful for detecting sounds and shapes, but goodness cannot be experienced in this way. So if what we call 'good' is the name of an invisible quality which we cannot touch or hear, just what do we mean, if anything, when we speak of that quality? If 'blue' is the name of all blue objects, or blue patches on objects, what is 'good' the name of?

All Good Things

One answer to this last question is the claim that just as 'blue' is the name of all blue things, so 'good' is the name of all good things. But there are objections to this view which are so overwhelming that most philosophers reject it as an answer to the problem. First, if we are to use a name properly it is essential that we all know to what the name refers. For example, it would be no use having the name 'tree' if some people meant by it 'all round objects' or 'all black objects'. This would lead to confusion in communication which would remain unresolved until it was agreed to use 'tree' to refer to one clear and distinct class of objects—say 'plants and large shrubs made from wood'. So with 'good' we must agree on which objects possess that quality, otherwise it will never be clear whether we are all using the word in the same way.

But secondly, having said all this, it is not necessary that we all agree which *objects* are good and which are bad (or at least 'not good'). It is necessary only that we have a list of the things or qualities which are good; for instance virtue, kindness, truthfulness etc. However, here is the crucial objection: even when we have agreed to call certain qualities 'good' it still makes sense to ask whether the incidence of one of these qualities in any particular situation is itself good. And if we can ask this question meaningfully, then it follows that no quality can unreservedly always be called 'good'. And it therefore follows that 'good' is not the name of a quality.

A more straightforward way of stating this is to say that since there is no universal agreement on just what makes any particular quality a good quality, then it is misleading to use the word 'good' to refer to a quality. In short, 'good' is not a name of anything even though it looks like a name.

If 'good' is not a name, then what is it?

A Satisfactory Compromise?

If 'good' is not the name of a quality, since whatever constitutes what 'good' refers to is neither touchable nor visible—and, crucially, its nature cannot be agreed upon, is the word 'good' something like an outburst of approval, a cheer? Some people have suggested that it is exactly this. To call something 'good', they say, is to recommend it or to say that you are in favour of it. You approve.

On this view, then, good is not a name or a description but an expression of recommendation. So if you call an action or a football match 'good' you are suggesting to everyone else that if they want to see or to perform a *good* action, to be a spectator at a *good* football match, then they ought to attend to the kind of action or match for which you cheer or to which you draw their attention. If we put this view into dialogue form, the difficulties behind its appealing appearance might become clear:

ALBERT: 'You ought to see Wanderers play; they're *good*.
BRIAN: Oh, I've not seen them; what do they do?
ALBERT: They have a strong defence and a very rugged approach to the game.
BRIAN: But what is particularly *good* about that?

So you see it's one thing to use 'good' as a commendation, a recommendation or a cheer but quite another to convey any particular meaning by so doing. For if the person you are talking with does not share your ideas about what is good, then he cannot agree with your commendation. What you call good might be regarded as bad to another. And since we are talking about meaning here, it is obvious that no clear sense of meaning is coming across where there is such disagreement. Notice as well that however much we want to take all description out of the meaning of good, it subtly returns (almost as a quality!) when anyone asks us *what* is good about something which we are recommending by our use of the word 'good'.

Let's Try to Agree

For such strong reasons we seem to have rejected all descriptive meaning to the word 'good'. We appear to have satisfactorily shown that 'good' is not the name of a quality. But, at the same time, it looks as though the suggestion that 'good' is a cheer or a commendation is by no means an ideal answer to our original question, because, sooner or later, any act of cheering seems to involve us in describing and putting a value on what we are cheering.

May we, then, suggest that the chief function of our use of 'good' is to show that we approve of a certain event or state of affairs, but that, in any particular case of which we approve, *there exist certain qualities* (or at least features) *which we are prepared to specify as being good?* This looks like a compromise, and perhaps it has some value. Can we clarify this conclusion further and suggest that when we use the word 'good' we mean to say two things:

(1) that we approve, commend or recommend something, and
(2) we are prepared to say *why, in any particular case,* we do approve commend, or recommend in terms of qualities or features of the object commended.

This is no final answer. It leaves much unsettled and, perhaps, even unsatisfactory. But, at least, it is an introduction to some of the difficulties in the meaning and use of what we might think to be a relatively simple word—'good'.

Exercise
(1) *Does the word 'good' mean anything? If so, what does it mean? If not, then why not?*
(2) *Are some things naturally good?*
(3) *If anything is naturally good, why do we say it is?*
(4) *What makes us want to call something 'good'?*
(5) *How would you teach a young child the meaning of the words 'good', 'beautiful' and 'lovely'?*
(6) *Is 'good' a cheer?*
(7) *Can we call something 'good' quite honestly and yet say we do not like it?*
(8) *Make a list of some good things.*
(9) *Give your opinion of the following:*
'Michael is honest and generous and kind, so, by any standards, he is a good person because no one can be honest, generous and kind and not be good'.
(10) *Is the fatal illness of a young child bad? If so, is a miraculous recovery good? Why or why not?*

10 Moral Philosophy

Morals and Authority

Why ought we to behave ourselves well? Why be good? It sometimes seems as if everyone is trying to persuade us to behave in a way of which they approve. Schoolteachers, parents, elder brothers and sisters tell us to be good. Politicians, preachers, leaders of the country encourage your parents to be good—to behave in the manner approved by them. Well, since we often resent these directions how to live our own lives, why should we take any notice of the people who are directing us?

Many answers are offered to this question 'Why be good?' One school of thought argues that we should be good because God says so. But, as you know from what we have discussed so far, this argument lacks all power to convince unless we have already accepted the authority of God for other reasons, or on other grounds. The same, of course, can be applied to 'the Bible', 'Moses', 'the Law' or any other supposed authority. The argument 'You must be good because the Bible says so', or 'because I say so' contains no logical power to persuade.

Utilitarianism

But what if an appeal is made to something that happens *as a result* of your good behaviour? For example: 'You should be good and then the class will learn its lessons properly and you will all do well in the exams'. This seems, even at first glance, to be a more reasonable and sound way of going about problems. To be good because of some command issued in the long dead past might seem pointless, but to be good so that some benefit will come of it in the future looks like a good idea. In this case let us define 'good' as 'keeping quiet order and attending to your books'. If you do this, then you and the rest of the class will do well. The teacher will be able to teach more and also more easily. This must be good for the examination prospects and general education of the class. I think there is hardly anyone who would want to find any major fault with the argument so far. But the problems begin to crop up when one or more members of the class think that they have a better reason than the class's examination success for behaving quite differently. We have defined good as being attentive and quiet. Now suppose one class member waves his arms about and shouts and points out of the window. According to our definition this would be thought to be extremely bad behaviour. It disrupts the lesson, upsets the teacher, and interrupts the material of the course. But consider two reasons for this disquieting behaviour:

(1) Atkinson jumps about noisily because it is nearly time to go home.
(2) Barker jumps about noisily because he has noticed that the tennis courts are on fire.

Isn't it likely that, at this point, most people would agree that while Atkinson's disruptive and bad behaviour was without good reason, Barker had a good excuse for overriding the rule about quiet and attentiveness? This is obviously an extreme example, and the decision to agree that Barker's conduct is better for the general good of the whole class, even the whole school, than remaining silent under the particular critical circumstances, will, I suspect, meet with the general approval. However, once we have said that Atkinson had no good excuse for his behaviour, but that Barker did act with good reason we are forced to deal with possible cases which fall between these two extremes. For instance, would standing up and shouting be in the general interest of the class if a member of it saw only smoke from the tennis court—smoke which usually comes from a fire lit by the gardener at this time of year? If so, why? If not, why not?

It was well said that it is the borderline cases, like that last mentioned which cause the most trouble in philosophy and particularly in that branch of philosophy which deals with human behaviour and the description of certain actions as 'good' and others as 'bad'.

Some philosophers argue that the rule such as 'Be quiet and attentive in class' ought never to be broken because, they say, any incident of rule-breaking is likely to weaken the tendency of the people to keep that good rule in the future. Sometimes these philosophers are called 'Rule Utilitarians'— 'rule' because they believe that rules are basic and necessary in human conduct, and 'utilitarian' because they base their theories not on commands or sacred books but on agreed desirable consequences or results. There is a straightforward objection to this point of view; and there is a rather more complicated one.

First, the straightforward argument against all utilitarian ideas of goodness and right conduct can be expressed forcefully in the question to the utilitarian. 'How do you know what the consequences of your act or of following your rule will be?' and 'How do you know that these consequences will be better for the people involved than other consequences, for example those resulting from the dictates or guidance of a holy book?' In these questions the objector is using, to further his argument, the fact that neither he nor the utilitarian can know the future. In this case the utilitarian, the believer in consequences, has at least two relevant replies. First he can claim to base his expectation of what will happen in the future, as a result of someone following his act or rules, on what has happened in similar cases in the past. And if the objector claims that *probable* happenings are not enough, the utilitarian is then presented with the neat knock down argument that the consequences of following the 'holy book' theory are also only probabilities. Just because the following of the guidance of a holy book has brought good consequences in the past is, by itself, no guarantee that it will do in the future, and particularly in the case in question. And the utilitarian can strengthen his own argument by the claim, based on observation and investigation of the facts, that this act is obviously more important for the production of good consequences than that of the Authoritarian objector. Weight is added to this argument if we make Barker, in the above example, a utilitarian and allow him to warn us of the fire!

There is a more subtle objection, however, to the Rule Utilitarian. Suppose he says: 'Good consequences come from following certain rules'. Let us say for example, giving money to earthquake disaster funds, telling the truth and keeping promises. Then suppose he says 'So we must always follow these rules'. An opponent of this view might say 'I am not an authoritarian, I believe, as you do, that consequences are the important elements in decisions about human conduct, but consequences depend not upon rules but upon *acts*'. Then let this new opponent, who wants partly to agree with the rule utilitarian, tell a story to illustrate his argument:

> There was once a ship sailing the Atlantic Ocean. It had a full crew and many women and children besides. Suddenly it became foggy, so the Captain issued the fog instruction 'always follow the compass'. Shortly after this instruction had been issued, the Chief Officer noticed a group of rocks straight ahead. He signalled that the ship's pilot ought to change direction. But the Captain interrupted with a repetition of the fog instruction, 'always follow the compass'. The Pilot ignored the Captain and, now seeing the rocks himself, put aside the compass and took evasive action based on his own judgement. There is no doubt that, had the fog instruction, always follow the compass' been followed, the ship would have run aground with a great loss of life.

It is plain to see that the new opponent of the Rule Utilitarian is suggesting very strongly by this exciting story that when it appears certain, or almost certain, that the following of a rule is going to lead to bad consequences, then the rule should be disregarded and the appropriate saving act undertaken. People who argue this point are, quite naturally, called Act Utilitarians. You see that they have much in common with the Rule Utilitarians in that they both believe in the overriding importance of consequences. The difference between them is that where one believes that good things come from following rules, the other claims that rules are sometimes inappropriate and fallible and so it is best to judge each case on its merits. It is interesting to note that in the case of the ship and the rocks, many Rule Utilitarians have argued that the Pilot ought still to have followed the compass even if so doing would have meant heavy loss of life. His reason for putting forward this apparently cold blooded idea is that any disobedience of a rule weakens the tendency of others to obey that rule on future occasions. And, since the rule *generally* promotes good consequences, it ought to be retained and always respected unweakened by any occasional floutings of its authority.

It may be that we think the Rule Utilitarian stubbornly in error on this very point, but it is doubtful whether this by itself proves the Act Utilitarian's case. For rulers are good general guides and certainly they seem more reliable than random acts and personal whim. But if there are occasions when the Rule Utilitarian has the correct prescription, and times when the right thing to do is that suggested by the Act Utilitarian, how is a neutral observer, who seeks only to prevent suffering and to increase happiness, to judge who is right on any particular occasion? This is a most difficult problem and it is doubtful whether there has ever been an entirely satisfactory solution to it. English Law is worth looking at here, for it makes an attempt to avoid the extremes of the two positions.

The law establishes a rule which is to be obeyed. But as time goes by and more and more infringements of the rule occur, the law modifies the rule to cover exceptional cases. For example the simple rule might, in the first place, be 'It is wrong to kill'. But what if one man kills another entirely in self defence—is that wrong? Or if another is killed by an accident? Suppose someone is faced with the horrible choice of either killing one man, and thus breaking the rule, or instead seriously injuring 359 others. What should he do in this case?

In practice the law 'recognizes' extreme examples of this kind and amends the rule in the light of circumstances so that, for instance, killing by accident or in self-defence is not regarded as such a serious breach of the rule as murder. This is how English law works. It bases the revision of its rules and judgements on actual cases. You may disagree; you might think this an immoral procedure. Certainly some philosophers are vaguely embarrassed by this method because if you look at it closely it does appear that, by qualification after qualification, amendment upon amendment, what began life as a Rule Utilitarian system collapses into Act Utilitarianism pure and simple!

White Lies

The problem of the exception to a good rule is highlighted by the idea of the white lie. You know the kind of thing: A favourite aunt bakes a cake which makes you sick. Are you to tell her, when she asks, how you vomited, or ought you rather to mumble that it was 'quite nice'? You have now recovered from the bout of sickness, besides you know that your aunt will be most upset if she learns she has caused any suffering. She lives alone and is liable to become depressed. Ought you to keep the moral rule 'Tell the truth' or, in this special case, should you tell a 'white lie'?

The Rule Utilitarian will advise you to keep the rule even if it means upsetting your aunt. He might argue: 'What would happen if *everyone* did the same as you, and lied when he thought he ought? We would never know when the truth was being told, and this would play havoc with our lives and with our society'. This may seem small comfort to you faced with the memory of billiousness and the prospect of a tearful aunt, but the Rule Utilitarian will argue that if you give in on this one and break the rule, it is but the thin end of the wedge, and soon the whole world will collapse in lies! The Act Utilitarian will console you with the promise that nothing so far reaching will occur by your simple piece of kind and considerate behaviour, and that it is obvious that your aunt must be spared suffering.

But as we saw in the example drawn from English law, only a very determined Rule Utilitarian would counsel you to tell the truth come what may. A softer Rule Utilitarian would say that in this particular case a lie is justified (because it avoids suffering and that is the purpose of Utilitarian theories). But this would bring a smile of triumph to the face of the Act Utilitarian, who would then claim that Rule Utilitarianism, once pronounced with such certainty and confidence, had collapsed, by way of its own arbitrary exceptions, into Act Utilitarianism. One thing is certain, agreement among moral philosophers is hard to discover!

Exercise
(1) *What can you argue against the view that an action is good because a holy book commands it?*
(2) *Why accept authority?*
(3) *Is there such a thing as a good action?*
(4) *Do you think that Rule Utilitarianism must collapse into Act Utilitarianism?*
(5) *Is any 'white lie' really white?*
(6) *If we judge acts by their consequences, how long do we have to wait, after the act, before we can say that its consequences were good?*
(7) *Should you always keep your promises?*

11 Aesthetics—A Question of Taste?

Have you noticed how some kinds of objects and activities are considered to be 'good' or 'good taste'? The idea of 'good taste' is widespread. Sometimes it seems to indicate things which are 'proper' or 'posh'—like setting out the knives and forks in a particular way, or preferring one motor car to another *simply* because of its name.

And it is not just 'high class' people or adults who go on about good and bad taste. Nearly all young people do the same. Except they do not always use 'good taste' or 'bad taste' but prefer to talk about 'the in thing' and are anxious to be 'hip', 'cool' or 'with it' and definitely not 'out', 'square' or in any other way unfashionable.

But is it simply a matter or fashion? What is good taste? And if we think we have discovered what good taste really is, are we obliged to try to acquire it? In trying to answer these questions it is a good thing to have a starting point, a place from which to view the whole scene. Let us take the law of the land as that starting place. It is worth noting that the law is completely indifferent to the way in which you set out the knives and forks, what kind of motor car you decide to buy (provided it is roadworthy) or whether you like rock music or soul. Nobody will try to have you locked up if you happen to prefer Mozart to Beethoven or Pink Floyd to The Rolling Stones.

If the law does not decide what is good or bad taste, then who does? Some people maintain that nobody does—that it is all a matter of personal choice and preference. Others are influenced by their friends or the 'in crowd'. Yet others put their faith in a special type of people called 'critics'. The critics give their views in journals or on the radio and television about the latest fashions in art, music and literature. How do they work?

The Critics at Work

Critics work by comparisons. They compare the work or object under review with similar works or objects which have passed into common knowledge. For example, if a writer submits a play with 'ambition' as its theme and ancient Rome as its location, then it is almost certain that that play will be compared with *Julius Caesar* a play by William Shakespeare on the same theme. Usually there are many plays and stories on any particular theme. The critics mention as many of these other works as they think are relevant to the play being reviewed. All the works with which new items are compared are 'classics' in the sense that they have passed into the common literary heritage. Although all classics are not necessarily good, there will always be at least a few intellectuals and critics to argue for each classic's superiority, so the comparisons always remain possible and likely.

Over the years style and mood change in literature. Once, long sentences, with many commas and semi-colons were the vogue; writers took great care over the construction of such sentences; they made them rhythmical and balanced. Short sentences are now the vogue. Critics note these gradual changes in style and mood and include them in their reviews. Most critics comment on bad logic and errors in reasoning as well. Thus an example of a short review might read:

Brave New Grandchildren—by Alexis Higgins
In this short novel of 188 pp Mr Higgins discusses the effects on human genetics of the planned and systematic use of insecticides on plants in maternity wards. His appreciation of the black comedy genre in apocalyptic novels is not so sure as Huxley's. It is inevitable that comparisons with Huxley's *Brave New World* will be made; the title as well as the subject matter guarantee that. But it would be unfair to draw too close a parallel between the two novels, especially since Higgins says in his short introduction that he is not interested in making a social comment, still less in issuing a prophetic warning. Besides the hero of *Brave New Grandchildren* is not the moral caricature of Huxley's 'savage'.

The crisp sentences in which the adventures of Higgins' *Dr Zhivlasto* serve to help the novel charge onwards with direction and purpose. However, when all antidotes to the evil Maldust's pollination clinics have been rather tortuously tried and chronicled, we are left feeling not quite certain at the end. Does Lemnia recover? How far are her children advanced in their plans to marry humans with plants? Mr Higgins leaves us in some doubt. Even if the Earth Mother psychology is rather over played at times, and the genetic consequences not clearly spelled out, we are left with an entertaining diversion for our holiday reading. We should accept it as such, not expecting a psycho-social tract.

Reviewers and critics, then, almost always relate any new offering to what has been generally accepted out of what has gone before. They relate to an *establishment* of previous literature and art. They write and talk in the fashionable jargon of the day—for instance 'Earth Mother' in the above review. Therefore critics are likely to be conservative—that is, it is probable and most likely that they will recommend the new works which are most similar in style or content to the accepted volumes. In this way tastes and styles are encouraged to change only very slowly. Sometimes it seems as though they do not change at all. This is not quite true, but you can gamble that the older a piece of literature, art, or music is the longer its period of fashion with the critics is likely to be. For example, Shakespeare wrote his plays about 400 years ago and I have never read a really bad modern review of Shakespeare. John Steinbeck wrote very recently, and I have read a few reviews of his work which are less than complimentary. So the longer a piece of work has belonged to the establishment, the more secure its place tends to become. In this way the critics become the people who say what good taste is—at least what good taste in art is.

11 Aesthetics   43

Avant Garde Critics

Having said all this, it would be a mistake to think that all critics are conservative and that they believe only old works to be good works. Of course, only a small number of contemporary books, paintings and musical compositions are likely to be of the very highest quality—only a small number of old works were judged to be excellent. In any generation some examples of art will be less good than others whatever the standard of evaluation chosen.

The Avant Garde Critics sometimes seem to be judging according to quite different criteria or standards from those employed by the regular critics. They seem to go out of their way to recommend artistic creations which appear to many people as unusual to say the least. What are we to make of the advice that we should regard a piece containing clanky sounds, similar (to the untrained ear) to the banging of several dustbin lids, as 'great music'? And should we think that the critic who raves about ☐☐ as a 'great new departure in art' has gone crazy?

I am not sure. But I do know that Avant Garde critics usually wish to assert that good music or painting of 'today' is bound to be different, at least in outward appearance, from what has gone before—or else it would be 'just a copy' and not a genuine work of art at all. These critics often reply to our outrage at the sight and sound of many modern offerings by telling us how the great masters of the past were also misunderstood in their own times and how many of them died in poverty.

Now the fact that a great artist was misunderstood in the eighteenth century does not guarantee that any aspiring painter, writer or musician who is misunderstood these days is therefore a great artist. If the critics want to suggest that as a compelling argument, then we should (by now!) find it easy to point to the fallacy in their reasoning. Actually no serious critic will try to persuade us by the use of such doubtful tactics. But the fact that not all great artists were accepted as such in their time, perhaps because they were misunderstood, ought to caution us against ruling out a modern work as worthless just because we cannot immediately see what the artist is trying to say.

There are a great many questions about art and the creative process. 'What is of value?', 'Which is second rate?', 'What is true originality?' and even 'Why do we prize originally in arts?'. These are issues of quite immense difficulty and we cannot go into them all here. But if we gain nothing else from the Avant Garde critics, we should learn not to reject any artistic creation, however unusual it may be, without first trying to get to grips with the artist's point of view or without the attempt to understand the evaluative criteria upon which favourable Avant Garde critics base their assessment of it.

I am sure you now enjoy may pieces of music which you were not at all fond of on first hearing. Often we learn to appreciate and grow to like paintings or songs through looking and listening over and over again. This fact may well account for the popularity of certain pieces of classical music which are used as introductions to television series. But are the critics really better judges than the rest of us?

The Critics' Authority

One reason for accepting the critics' opinion is that they are learned men and are good at comparisons in art and literature and therefore 'know' what is good and what is shoddy. There is a straightforward objection to this argument. 'How do the critics support their claim to dictate to us what is good or poor not just in new works but even among the classics'? In other words it may be asked why anyone *must* like Shakespeare. It is by no means certain that there is any satisfactory answer to this objection. One attempt to answer it says that we ought to like (or at least acknowledge the quality of) the classics because their quality stands out, it is obvious. This is, of course, to say to the man who claims not to be aware of the alleged obvious nature of this quality that he is culturally blind, that he has no sense for literature, no ear for music or whatever else the case may be. From this point, the argument can easily develop into an angry row. People do not like being told that they are culturally blind any more than they like being told they are ugly or idiotic. Consequently they lash back at the critic with expressions like 'snob', 'pseud' and 'elitist rubbish'.

Critics, and (let's not just blame them alone) all others who defend the cultural establishment can, when they have recovered their composure after such attacks on their own good taste, make an appeal like 'Well, even if *you* do not see the value of Shakespeare, all the Professors of English Literature and a good majority of all intelligent people do'. This is familiar ground to you, by now. You will recognize it instantly as a fallacious argument which fails because it appeals to an authority not necessarily accepted by everyone.

When this argument is shown to be fallacious the defenders of good taste are not high and dry. They have another approach; they can appeal to certain technical aspects of the work of art in question. For example, in the case of say, a Piano Concerto in C minor by Mozart, they might argue 'No one can combine classical form and romantic emotion so well as Mozart does in this piano work'. But this is not convincing. It is perfectly fair to offer two arguments in reply. First, an outright disagreement of fact claiming that the work is trivial: 'Beethoven did much better things with form and emotion in his C minor concerto'. Secondly, one may grant the accuracy of the factual assertion that no one can combine form and emotion as well as Mozart can, but then proceed to argue that that in itself has little or even nothing to do with the quality of a piece of work. So Mozart has such an excellent combination of form and emotion? If you or I do not like classical form or romantic emotion, then Mozart is not one of our favourite composers, and we are under no obligation to regard his work as possessing a superior quality before which we must bow.

Is Criticism Professional Snobbery?

Is it possible, then, that the views of the cultural establishment are a kind of unspoken conspiracy designed to perpetuate the notion of the quality versus the rubbish—the quality being what they prefer; the rubbish left for us? More, is it even possible that the debate is like the story by Hans Andersen of the King's new clothes? Will some innocent person one day let the cat out of the bag and proclaim that, after all, the arguments of the establishment are all wind and water? And will good taste then crumble into an obvious facade?

It is very likely that neither of these two ends will occur. There is perhaps something to be said for and against the notion of good taste, especially in art and literature. In favour may be suggested the cynical opinion that even if all the classics are really rubbish after all, we still need to be familiar with them so that we can share in the conversations of the establishment and cause others to think us cultured and full of good taste. This is the exclusive club mentality. Learn to talk about the classics and everyone will think you are clever, cultured, educated, desirable etc. This seems hypocrisy and an ignoble reason for professing good taste. It makes good taste into bad taste.

A more positive argument in defence of the classics as good taste is the one which suggests that if we acquaint ourselves with them and bury ourslevs in study of them then we shall ourselves live more meaningful lives—presumably because in the classics we come across the best and noblest, the loftiest and deepest of human emotions and ideas. But the most that can be said in defence of this is that if *your* life is improved by becoming familiar with the classics, good *for you*. Who is to say what counts as an improvement in anyone's life? Someone else might claim that eating egg and chips improved his life immeasurably! True enough, by becoming familiar with the classics our knowledge is increased—at the very lowest level we know more stories, more pieces of music etc. But who is to put a value on such familiarity? One who wishes to argue against the establishment can still ask what significance this knowledge or familiarity has for him. As we saw in an earlier chapter all appeals by the establishment to certain esteemed groups such as to 'the majority of educated people' cannot, logically, force us to bow to their arguments. It is possible that on this one issue of good taste the majority of intelligent people are wrong.

The Pop Establishment

It would be misleading to imagine that the critic, and indeed all evaluation in art, is concerned only with so called 'high brow' topics like Shakespeare and Mozart, Leonardo and Bach. If you read the popular weekly musical papers you will find comments and criticisms of all kinds of pop music. Even the 'serious' Sunday papers carry a pop column. Light hearted theatrical comedy shows and television revues are the subject of just as much conversation among devotees as symphony concerts are among lovers of 'classical' music.

Back in Chapter 6 we saw that we always need to qualify the word 'exists' by reference to a context or an area of discourse. For example, 'Americans exist *in Texas*', 'Unicorns exist *in mythology*', 'Ghosts exist *in the works of Shakespeare*', etc. So it is with the word 'classic'. There are classics of popular music—The Beatles' 'Eleanor Rigby' for instance—and classics of television comedy—perhaps Tony Hancock's 'The Blood Donor'—besides the classics of so-called 'high brow culture'. It is just as much a mistake to try to compare Pink Floyd with Brahms as it is to put Americans and unicorns in the same category.

Perhaps each classic and great work of art, entertainment or culture is so designated as a result of the enthusiastic acclaim with which it is received by devotees of *a particular and relevant* area of art, entertainment or culture. After all, it is likely that Mick Jagger, the pop star, is better placed than Dr F. R. Leavis, the literary critic, to say which new rock and roll single will be a hit!

Summary

Perhaps in the end we need to add a word of caution. As we saw in the chapter about existence, it is misguided to ask whether something 'really' exists, so in the case of good taste it may be equally doubtful and pointless to enquire whether the classics really are of good quality. For after a while it becomes obvious that such an enquiry is by no means as straightforward as it once appeared. In the end *just what kind of question are we asking here*? If we are asking 'Is what has been called "good taste" really "good taste"?' then we are asking something like 'Does what exists really exist'? And we know by now the many objections to that question. If we are asking 'Is *this* quality and is *that* rubbish'? then it may be that we can answer this question only by accepting some authority or other, be it of the Arts Council or of our own learning.

Exercise
(1) *Can a critic earn his money honestly in the business of criticism?*
(2) *Argue with some friends the point*
    'Shakespeare is better than Alexis Higgins'
(3) *Can the technical qualities of a piece of work allow us to call that work good or bad?*
(4) *'Good taste is nothing but the preferences of the rich'—do you agree?*
(5) *'Tastes change so it is possible that something which was once thought to be good taste is now bas taste. Therefore there are no such things as good and bad taste'. Is this a convincing argument against good taste?*
(6) *In the end do I myself decide what is good taste and what is bad taste?*
(7) *Make your own list of things which are in good taste.*

12 The Problem of Meaning—Part Three

Fallacies
There are even more ways of being wrong than those we have covered already. You may find this hard to believe, but some of these mistakes are made so frequently that they have been given names. They are called Formal Fallacies. Imagine being wrong FORMALLY! We ought to look at them, so that we may guard against falling into these particular traps.

Some not All
This mistake is made when we apply to a whole group of people or objects characteristics which we ought strictly to apply only to a part of that group. For example, look at the following argument:
(1) All schoolboys are forbidden to play ball in the yard.
(2) Mary Thomas is playing ball in the yard.
(3) Therefore she is doing what is forbidden.
But she's not, you know. (3) does not follow from (1) and (2); you can see why. Mary Thomas does not belong to the class of people who are forbidden, becasuse she is a girl and therefore not a schoolboy. Once again we have chosen a straightforward example and it would be wrong to imagine that the argument's faults are always as obvious as this. Sometimes the fallacy or mistake is very well concealed—especially by those people who use all kinds of methods to persuade us to accept their point of view.

In a Circle
Here is an error which is sometimes very difficult to spot, usually because the argument which contains it is extremely long and complicated. Once more, though, here is a simple example: 'The Bible is all true because it says so in the Bible'. You might think that no one would make so silly a mistake, but I have heard, and even read, this sentence as a defence of the view that there are no errors in scripture. It is a mistake to argue in a circle like this because no evidence is offered in the second part of the argument for the point which you make in the first part. No attempt to justify the statement first made succeeds when we argue in a circle. We are simply saying 'It's true because it's true', 'A = A'. 'A married man is a man' etc.... We are providing no new evidence to back up the point which we make. So, avoid arguing like this and be especially careful not to be misled by more complicated examples of the same mistake. *That's what the man said* is almost the same sort of error that we talked about earlier when we said that it is incorrect to accept the conclusions of an argument just because it is argued by an impor-

tant or approved figure or famous group of people such as 'the Archbishop' 'the Professor' 'all honest men' etc.... Remember, what counts is the structure of the argument and not the status of the man who argues it.

But the fallacy 'That's what the man said' is slightly different from the earlier example, though it is still a fallacy. It consists of saying something like 'Brown says we should obey the law, but I know he was caught for speeding, so his argument is worthless'. His argument is not worthless simply because he failed on one occasion to do what he believes we all (including himself) ought always to do. There are many variations of this mistake, but they all boil down to the same basic error—that of attacking a person instead of the person's argument.

Time and Cause

This is very common. It is the mistake of arguing that because one thing happened before another thing, then that first event *caused* the second. I have a personal and, I think, classical example of this error. My grandfather, wanting to advise me against eating oysters, told me the cautionary tale of a man he knew who ate a plateful of oysters, retired to bed and then died. Now it may be that the oysters killed him, but my grandfather offered no evidence for this belief. He seemed to assume that, because death followed oyster eating, eating oysters was the cause of death. Perhaps he was just playing a verbal trick. The fact remains that the mistake of calling prior events 'causes' is very common.

These fallacies, errors and mistakes are not always so easily spotted as in the obvious examples I have used. I have said this before, but it can hardly be said too often because frequently they are hidden in long and complicated arguments where they are rarely detected at first glance.

Exercise
(1) Give one example of each of the four types of fallacy in this chapter.
(2) What is a fallacy?
(3) Can you argue correctly by accident? Explain, please.
(4) 'It rained last Friday, and it is Friday today, so it will rain today'. Is this a fallacy? If so, what kind?
(5) All iron bars sink.
This sinks.
This, then, an iron bar.
Is there anything wrong with this argument? If so, what?
(6) Give the fallacy in question 5 a name.
Make up a similar example of your own.

13 Causation

In the last chapter we had a closer look at common fallacies. One of them was the assumption that, because one event happened before another then the first event caused the second. We saw how this is often a mistake. But there are occasions when we want to talk about causes. We do believe that events are caused, don't we? If you prick someone, surely he will bleed; if I drop something, surely it will fall?

It may seem amazing, but the ideas that pricking someone causes him to bleed or dropping something causes it to fall have been doubted. Men have argued that the occurrence of one event before another, even when the first *seems* to cause the second, is not a good enough reason for belief in any cause. This appears to be sound advice when we remember the man who ate oysters and died, but surely we would want to argue with such doubt, when we come to cases involving pricking and bleeding, or dropping a heavy weight and the weight falling.

But even these have aroused doubt. First it has been argued that when we claim to observe cause and effect in, for example, the incident 'Man drops brick: brick falls' we are really only seeing a coincidence. Even when we see this incident happen over and over again, we are told that we cannot prove the existence of a cause so we must continue to limit our description of the incident to coincidence. We protest of course, but can we prove the existence of a cause here?

Well, if we are to say that the event 'dropping a brick' (call it *A*) caused the event 'the brick falling' (call it *B*) we must find the cause in the event which happened first—dropping the brick. We call event *A* 'the cause' and event *B* 'the effect' or 'the result'. Now, if we want to say '*A* caused *B*' then we must say that the cause is in *A*. Otherwise it would be difficult to say clearly what '*A* caused *B*' really means. So we must examine the event *A* and try to discover in it a cause. But when we look at *A* what do we see? A hand dropping a brick? Yes. Any particular thing which we can call 'a cause'? No. Only a hand, a brick and perhaps a person. We cannot point to anything and say 'That is a cause'.

However, we continue to take the fact of causes for granted. We live all our lives on the basis that if one thing happens then another particular thing will happen. If we did not assume the fact of causes we should not be able to plan or regulate our lives at all. We must be able to make statements, about water (for instance that you can drown in it) which become guides to everyday living. And we do observe certain regularities in the world, don't we? Everything does not appear to occur in a totally haphazard way. If we drop something we can bet on the fact that it will fall; if it rains the pavement will get wet.

But when we are asked to point to the cause of any event, proof that there are causes soon becomes a difficult task. This is because any agent or occurrence which we suggest is acting as a cause my be discounted as quite an irrelevant feature by someone else. If we believe in causes, the job of proving that they exist and of saying what they are belongs to us. Notice that we have been thinking all the time of causes as occurrences which we can or ought to be able to point to. This is where we have our difficulty. This is where we find it hardest to go against the philosopher who does not believe in causes. We cannot 'see' a cause in the same way that we 'see' an apple, so our task of finding proof that there are causes is made harder. Suppose we try another approach to the problem.

Remember how we were able to describe something as 'good'. We accepted the idea that 'good' is not the name of a particular quality or aspect of a thing; it is more like a word we use especially to say that we approve of a certain thing. Remember also that we said 'good' is not just a cheer. If we call anything 'good' we must be able to go on and say why it is good. Well, perhaps the word 'cause' is a bit like the word 'good'. It may be that just as we cannot point to what we say is good about an object, yet we know how to use the word 'good' so we can do the same with 'cause'. When we use the word 'cause' we are understood. We can communicate by this word. Look at these sentences:

(1) 'Going out half dressed in the rain caused him to catch cold.'
(2) 'The cause of England's footballing failure was lack of confidence.'
(3) 'I slipped on the banana skin and that caused me to fall.'
(4) 'The sun causes the flowers to grow.'
(5) 'The voters caused the downfall of the government.'

In all five examples, the word 'cause' is used. But so far from it being mysterious, it appears as a commonplace, a word understood clearly in each context. From this we might argue that to look for a cause in the same way that you might look for a slipper is to make a mistake at the start. We might say "Cause" is a word like "good". It does not name anything visible to our senses but it has a meaning'.

Very well. But if we are to say that 'cause' is like 'good', if it has a meaning, we must say just how it actually works, how it means, how it is used. Perhaps we can say that the idea of cause, like the comparable idea of good, is not drawn from the observation and naming of a quality but from the need to generalize, evaluate, measure or pass an opinion on a series of events. And through the process of more and more generalizations, measurements and opinions, we arrive at a clear and realistic use of the word 'cause'. You might say that our own idea of causes and their effects helps us to understand the world in a more precise and definite way. It is obviously an advantage to be able to talk about causes and effects especially with regard to the future. I mean, if we can say to a friend, 'If you do this, then that or the other will happen'; we have told him something useful. The point to grasp is that we have made this useful comment by employing the idea of causes. Once again, as in the case of 'good', we have used a word sensibly without having to get involved in misleading debates about what visible thing the word refers to. We can say 'Causes do not exist in the world; we use the idea of cause to understand the world'.

Some philosophers would like to argue even further—that the idea of 'cause' and 'effect' is essential to our thought, to the way we think. They say that we can no more do without the idea of cause than we can ignore basic concepts like 'up' and 'down', 'black' and 'white'. I am not sure just how necessary the idea of cause is to our understanding of the world. Perhaps we might have evolved and developed in such a way that we should have had no use for the ideas of cause and effect. The fact is that we didn't. And if you talk to anyone, even a fairly young child, about causes, you will be understood. That seems to matter much more than the puzzle of what we are *pointing to* when we use the word 'cause'.

Final Cause?

Sometimes people say, 'It's for a good cause'. They say this particularly when they have to give some money or put up with a certain amount of hardship, for instance poppy day or saving for an annual holiday. It seems, at first sight, difficult to think of the events of which they are speaking here as causes. This is because these events seem to be the results of a series of events rather than their causes. But a little thought sorts this one out. It is only *because* I save up all year that I can have a holiday in August. So it looks as if there is something about my holiday which causes the events which go before it. But this is not the way in which we normally use the word 'cause'. This is not how you would be understood if you started to talk about causes. So are there different kinds of causes? Some people have said that there are, and that this latter sort are called 'final causes'. In our example, the holiday in August is the final cause of my saving for the rest of the year. This is understandable in one sense: my intention of going on holiday in August might be strong enough to cause me to deny myself a few luxuries during the rest of the year.

But this is usually not all that users of the phrase 'final causes' mean by it. They often mean to suggest the presence of *purpose*. Religious people sometimes use the idea of final causes. 'All things work together for the glory of God' is a good example of a religious view of the events in the world. Whether there is any such final purpose or end to which all things in the world are being drawn, is, of course, a matter of opinion. But it is clear that we do not usually use the word 'cause' to refer to this final purpose. We do not, as a rule, use the word 'cause' to indicate *results*; more often we use it to refer to what produces the results. But it is worth mentioning this more informal use of the word 'cause' simply because we do, sometimes, use the word in this way. We must remember both to entertain all reasonable doubts about future events being the cause of present actions, and to bear in mind that we normally use the word 'cause' to indicate quite a different kind of occurrence.

Exercise

(1) *'I cannot see a cause, so I don't believe in causes'.*
Comment.
(2) *Is there anything in the slipperiness of the banana skin which causes me to fall when I tread on it? If so, what? If not, why do I fall?*
(3) *What do we mean when we say that something caused something else?*
(4) *Can anything which happens in the future cause something which happens in the past?*
(5) *What is wrong with the following:*
'Some creatures who understand a language wear hearing aids.'
Dolphins are creatures which understand a language.'
'So, dolphins wear hearing aids.'
(6) *'He got his feet wet, so he was sure to have caught a cold'.*
Is there anything wrong with this argument? If so, what is wrong with it?
(7) *'The lightning always occurs before the thunder, so the lighting causes the thunder.' Does it?*

14 Definition

So far we have talked as if the word 'meaning' itself had a clear meaning. It sounds to be a terrible complication to suggest that we are not always clear what we mean by 'meaning'. But such complications and puzzles are part of the everyday diet in philosophy; and attempts to unravel them can be good fun.

Ostensive Definition (1)—Pointing and Talking

In one sense of the word, meaning is a method of discovering the names of objects which we can actually see and point to. We learn most of these names when we are very young. They are the names of commonplace objects like tables and chairs, cups and saucers. The method is a simple one: someone points to a chair and says aloud the word 'chair'. So we are supposed to learn names. Even with a simple method, however, it is not always possible to avoid mistakes. I mean, suppose someone is trying to teach me the meaning of 'chair', and imagine that I have never before seen a chair. Now when someone points to an ordinary armchair and says to me 'chair' how do I know that it is the entire and complete object which is being referred to? I might, quite legitimately since I have never seen a chair, think that the teacher is trying to teach me the name of a colour to which he is pointing, or that the word 'chair' is an expression of surprise, a greeting or a complaint. Of course, we can often make a good guess at a speaker's meaning by his facial expression, tone of voice etc, so this kind of mistake is not made very frequently. The fact remains that mistakes are sometimes made, and we fail to understand on some occasions that a process of naming is going on.

What happens when we make this kind of mistake? First, if we make it when we are just beginning to learn language, when we are very young, then we simply remain puzzled or in error until, after many more repetitions of the same situation, we begin to associate the word 'chair' with actual chairs. If we make the same mistake about some new object to which we are being introduced when we are older, and are able to speak our native language, then we can be corrected immediately. For instance 'No, no, the gadget in the box is called a microscope, the thing on the end of the tube is a bunsen burner'.

Perhaps we can say then that sometimes meaning is talking and pointing. We learn names in this way. And sometimes, of course, we can substitute pictures and writing for pointing and talking. For example:

= 'man' or ☼ = 'sun'.

This is a basic way of learning meanings, but it is not the only way. Other ways of learning meanings exist simply because words are used to mean in more ways than one.

Ostensive Definition (2)—Defining the Invisible

Sometimes we cannot point to an object which is the meaning of a word, or which that word stands for. 'Ouch!' is a good example. If someone bangs his leg and says 'Ouch!' we cannot point to his leg and say that it is the meaning of 'ouch'. Nor is his pain the meaning; neither is the total accident what he means when he shouts, in pain, 'Ouch!' Can we point to anything then, and say with any conviction 'This is what "Ouch!" means?' Well, if we proceed in the same way as we did in the section on talking and pointing, we would expect there to be some object called 'an ouch'. Let us examine the accident, that is, let's point to the total number of events that make up the accident and see if we can detect anything which might be an ouch. The main characters seem to be:

(1) the unfortunate person involved;
(2) his leg;
(3) the chair;
(4) his shout 'ouch!';
(5) the victim's pain.

Now we can eliminate most of these objects and events fairly simply. The person involved is not called 'ouch!' He has a proper name. The pain is not 'ouch'; it is suffering, ache, shock or whatever. No one uses 'ouch!' to name a pain. In a very straightforward sense, of course, 'ouch!' is the shout of pain or annoyance, but this does not tell us the whole truth about the meaning of that shout. To know the whole story we must make a comparison with 'talking and pointing'. One of the skills, perhaps the main skill, with which this method of learning equips us is the ability to recognize the same thing (or a similar thing) on all future occasions. That is once we have learned the meaning of 'man' or 人 we do not forget how to use and apply the word. So we use the word 'man' accurately and consistently throughout our lives. We say '"Man" has a meaning. It is a word which enables us to talk about human beings of one sex'. We use 'man' appropriately whenever we use the word in this area of conversation.

Are there similar parallel occasions when we use the word 'ouch' accurately and consistently? 'Man' is always used in the presence of a man (or men) or in accompaniment with the idea of man (or men). It is not simply used to teach the meaning of itself in talking and pointing—that would be absurd. It is used, by people who have once learned its meaning to discuss man. So 'ouch' is used in connection with occasions of accident or pain. But it is not used in the same way as 'man' is used, and to this extent we may say that it means in a different way, its meaning is understood differently, or that people use a different method of meaning when they say 'ouch!' 'Man' is used to name, to describe, to discuss and to define. 'Ouch!' is used to express, to appeal, and as a reaction; sometimes as an involuntary reaction. It is a shorthand message. It means 'I am in pain' or 'It hurts'. It is not the name of anything, but it is the right and appropriate accompaniment of certain particular situations—pain situations. In this way it functions like a shout of joy, a cheer, a laugh or a grunt. But just because its meaning cannot be trimmed down to one object or class of objects like 'men' or 'chairs' we are not to imagine that we may be casual or even careless in our use of 'ouch!' and similar words. They do not name objects, but they belong to specific events in human life. There are occasions when it would be wrong to use them. 'Ouch' is out of place when uttered by someone enjoying chocolate cake. 'Yum' might here be a suitable verbal gesture. So we must note that in order to have meaning a word does not need to name an object. It can still convey a very definite message. How do we learn the meaning of 'ouch!'? Curiously, we learn it in exactly the same way as we learn the meaning of 'man'—by hearing it in a particular context and associating it with particular events of a specific nature.

Synthetic Definition

When we get to understand more words, we are able to use a different, and speedier, way of increasing our knowledge of meanings. We have seen that, to get to know basic meanings like those of 'red' or 'hard' it is easiest to point and talk—to associate a particular word with a particular thing. But if we know what 'side' means, if we have learned the correct usage of 'plane' and 'figure' then, given one or two everyday words like 'a' and 'by' we are able to discover the meaning of triangle. We can understand both:

△ is a triangle
'triangle' means △

and 'triangle' means a plane figure bounded by three sides. You can see instantly that this is a much more efficient method of learning meanings of new words than that which involves us in a searching out particular examples. It may be that the benefit of this method is not immediately apparent in examples like 'triangle' or 'red' but the advantage is obvious in a case like 'symphony'. Because there are more words like 'symphony' than there are words like 'red' the number of meanings which we are able to learn without referring directly to objects is very great. Besides it is often much simpler to use words we know than to point and talk when we are seeking to discover new meanings. Take the example 'symphony'. It would be very difficult to convey the meaning of this word by pointing and talking. What would we point at? An orchestra? But then perhaps we are misunderstood (quite naturally) to mean by 'symphony' the people and instruments of the orchestra. May we point to the musical score? With only limited success, for once again we could easily be misunderstood to mean the actual manuscript copy—the solid book of music.

But if we say '"Symphony" means in its classical form, a piece of music in four parts or movements for orchestra' then we stand a much better chance of being understood. This method of teaching or learning words is called 'synthetic definition'. The only disadvantage in this way of learning meanings is that we need a good basic stock of words already. We need a good vocabulary. But once we learn some words, it becomes easier to learn others. In short, the more words you know the more words you can easily get to know. And if we believe that there is knowledge contained in the grammatical formulation of words and sentences, then the more words we know, the more knowledgeable we shall become. We shall be able to build up more pictures of the world.

Exercise

(1) *Explain how you would teach the meaning of the following words*:
  (a) *'Apple'*.
  (b) *'Gap'*.
  (c) *'Treason'*.
(2) *When is it best to use the talking and pointing method of indicating meanings?*
(3) *Give examples, from different areas of life, where the meaning of a word is not something to which we can point.*
(4) *Why learn more words?*
(5) *What does 'meaning' mean?*
(6) *Which kinds of words are the most difficult to learn? Why?*
(7) *When is it best to use the 'Using words to teach the meaning of words' method? Give examples.*
(8) *How would you explain the meaning of 'atmosphere' to*
  (a) *a group of 7 years old;*
  (b) *a class of intelligent adults.*

15 The Existence of God

A Recurring Question

In this section we shall be a little more detailed in our observation and analysis than we have been in earlier chapters. This is not because the existence of God is necessarily a more important topic than any other, nor because I think that I have any easy or clear answer to it—I do not. But the question of God's existence has been touched on by all the major philosophers of the last 2500 years. Many, including Aristotle, Aquinas, Descartes, Berkeley, Hume and Kant—giants among philosophers—have dealt with this subject in great detail.

Besides, the existence of God is a subtly different kind of question from others we have looked at. It is more speculative. That is to say, it does not matter whether you believe that the world is as it appears; as we saw earlier you would fall through a sense-datum of thin ice with just as much ease as you would fall through 'real' thin ice. The answer to the question 'Is there anything there?' when applied to the world, leaves everything as it is. It makes no difference to the way we live whether we are phenomenalists or realists.

But if we come to the conclusion that there is a God who creates and maintains the world and has a purpose for his creation, then we might regulate our conduct quite differently from the way we would behave if we concluded that the universe originated by accident and is without ultimate purpose. In this sense problems of theology (about God) are similar in kind to problems about ethics (behaviour).

As I said, there is no easy answer to this question, but it is a useful and interesting exercise to take a look at part of the history of the idea of God and at some arguments for and against his existence.

History of the Idea of God—One Approach

Is there a God? Men have asked this question for hundreds of years. They have disagreed about how it ought to be answered. They have fought wars with those who have held opinions different from their own. Some say that more human misery has been caused by the idea of God than by anything else. This last sentence alone is enough to start an argument if not a war. But perhaps the question, 'Is there a God?' is too vague. Many people believe greatly differing things about God; so it is possible to say that really they are talking about different gods. At least we may be sure that many different meanings are given to the word 'God'. What do you mean by it? Do you use the word? How do you understand it?

Some mean by 'God' a sort of Spirit which exists in all people. Others think that God is the maker of all that exists. Still others believe that there are many gods. It is even worth mentioning that many people treat material objects as if they were gods. For instance, the television and the motor car. It is not only primitive and uneducated people who create idols.

It is obvious that, if we are to be able to discuss the question of God's existence sensibly, we must begin with a definition, or at least a rough and ready account of what we mean by the word 'God'. Let us take as our example then what most English or Western people mean by 'God'. Let us say, 'God is a being or a power not created by man; rather he made man; he made the universe and is in control of it. He also governs and directs what will ultimately become of us. He is unlimited in power and intelligence and knowledge. He does not exist as men exist, but he is an invisible spirit. God has always existed and will always be. Also, he is completely good'.

Now why should we think that such a being exists? There are at least two ways of looking at this question. First, 'How did belief in such a being arise?' and secondly, 'Is it a reasonable belief? It is important to keep these two questions quite distinct from each other. The way in which we come to believe a particular thing to be true has nothing to do with whether that thing is true. For example, I might have accepted that $3 \times 3 = 9$ after having been beaten with a stick by an impatient teacher. But being beaten, though a *cause* of my belief that $3 \times 3 = 9$, is not a *good reason* for believing the truth of this piece of arithmetic. To put this another way, we might say that beating does not cause the truth that $3 \times 3 = 9$. It may cause a sore backside! Perhaps we can express this with greater accuracy and say that the truth of a belief is quite independent of the way by which we become convinced of the truth of that belief. The world is not round because the teacher says so; it is round because of certain facts which have to do with astronomy and other branches of science.

So, to take the first question first, 'How did belief in God arise?' This is a question which can be answered by the historian—the person who can refer to ancient tribal customs and beliefs—the man to whom the past is, if not an open book, at least accessible to study and method. Perhaps the student of history will tell us that our very advanced and complicated view of God comes from a belief which was, to begin with, primitive and simple. Maybe something like a thunderstorm, an earthquake, darkness or a sunrise in the first place convinced people that there is a God. Certainly, primitive people with little knowledge of science would find the idea of a controlling spirit or being quite a reasonable cause of many events which we tend to interpret in a scientific way. Gradually our idea of God has grown up, has matured, and in the twentieth century we have a very complicated point of view about God and the world. It does not matter that this educated opinion began as superstition or that it developed from an extremely primitive and irrational notion. The fact is that belief in God exists as a definite option for anyone to take. Now we must look at the second question which asks whether this belief is reasonable.

God as Creator of Everything?

Some people argue that God must exist in order for the universe to exist. Since the universe does exist there must be a God. Those who believe this usually wish to claim that God made all that there is ... 'In the beginning, God made the heaven and the earth'. Their argument rests mainly on a deep dislike for an unending series of events; so to complete the series, in what is thought to be the only reasonable way, they introduce the idea of God. God comes at the end of the following list:

(1) My parents made me.
(2) My grandparents made my parents.
(3) Primitive man evolved from the apes.
(4) The apes came from extremely simple creatures.
(5) All life evolved very slowly from inorganic matter.
(6) The earth broke off from the sun.
(7) The sun is a part of an old galaxy.
(8) The galaxy is a part of the universe.
(9) The universe began with clouds of hydrogen atoms.
(10) God made the hydrogen.

So it is suggested that God is the creator of all that there is—that the whole of creation depends for its existence upon God. Sometimes the argument is put as crudely as this, though frequently a more refined version of it is suggested. The more refined version says that God is continually creating, upholding and sustaining the world. He did not simply begin it all—like a referee starting a football match with a blast on a whistle. No. God is always active in supporting and renewing the universe and all that is in it. Both versions do in fact make the same point; the world is not an independent, self-governing thing. It requires the care and power of an Almighty Creator to keep it going. Well, does it?

Certainly there is something rather neat about this argument. It answers the question, 'Where did we all come from?' in a neat and straightforward way. It provides a resting place for restless minds. When we wonder and puzzle about the origin of all things we need only introduce the idea of God and our puzzlement disappears. But does it? Many would say it does not. For what have we done by adding God to the end of our list in the account of how things came to be? Perhaps we have only added one more item to the list—God. And if we can add one item, then what is to stop us from adding another? We can sensibly ask the question, 'Who made God?'.

Sometimes this move is resisted by some believers who argue that God is not just one more item in the list, he is the maker of the list. He is eternal, all powerful and all good. But we may reply, 'We do not know that he is any of these things until we know he exists. Give us first proof of his existence'.

After all anyone can claim the existence of anything that takes his fancy. We need a *reason* for belief in God and not just a definition of what God might be like *if* he existed. In fact the believer who uses the Creator argument for the existence of God is really saying: 'I am not satisfied with an endless series of events. Someone or something must be the cause of these events. I call that cause God'. So we see that this is not a logical argument at all. It is the preferred view of the believer who uses it. It may of course be right; it may be wrong. But we are not compelled by logic or necessity to accept it.

After criticizing the 'explanation' argument so fiercely it is only fair to say that we do perhaps have good reason for this kind of argument to be upheld and accepted. In most of our daily dealings we talk about causes and effects, so surely it is reasonable to assume that the universe has a cause as well. This is where, measuring the evidence, you must make up your own mind. A famous philosopher, Bertrand Russell, has said that because we believe events in the world have causes, this is no reason for believing that the whole world has a cause. Is 'no reason' rather too strong here? I don't know. Enough to say there are strong arguments on both sides, though both seem to be built more upon personal opinion and preference than on logic and sound reason. Pay your money; take your choice.

The Argument from Design

There is an argument for the existence of God which points to *order* and *sequence* in the world claiming that God is responsible for this. It is argued that the orderly succession of night and day, winter and summer, sunshine and rain is due to the design of God. And it is said that God planned the happy and convenient balances which exist in the world: not too hot to fry us all; not too cold to freeze us to death. Enough food and water, though not too much water or else we drown. A more or less equal number of men and women, a good supply of necessary minerals etc. You can try to list other examples of order in the universe.

At first glance it looks as if the world has been designed with all the care that a watchmaker takes when making a watch. So this argument rests not simply on the fact that something exists, but that something *special* exists, something delicate and patterned. And the aim of the argument from design is to show that such a complicated pattern could not have occurred by accident. God is needed to create such fine order.

We ought to ask many questions of this argument. Perhaps the first, 'Is it really such a well designed world?' Sure enough there appears to be much in the world that is orderly, like the sequence of darkness and light, but is there not also a great deal of disorder and chaos? Most of us are fortunate enough to escape death by drowning, but many people die each year in floods. There are also great droughts and earthquakes. Much of the earth's surface is desert and wasteland. It does not look as if this has been planned very carefully. Much of what exists seems to show proof of chaos rather than evidence of design. So we may argue that it is within the scope of an all powerful God to create and design a perfect world; and since the world is perfect we do not have *this* particular argument for belief. At least, if the argument relies for its appeal on a well-designed world, then the absence of good design crucially weakens the argument.

There is the further point that, even if the world appeared to be well-designed, this would not prove the existence of God. It would not of course prove anything. At the most a well-designed world would *suggest* the existence of a designer. And a designer is not necessarily the same thing as an everlasting and all powerful God. The designer, if he ever existed, may now be dead. So the argument from design cannot prove the existence of the kind of God believed in by any of the great religions of the world.

Remember what we discussed in the section on causes. There it was suggested that cause does not exist *in* the world, but the idea of cause is brought by us to the world so that we can make better sense of what we experience. The idea of cause helps us in the same way as spectacles help a man with poor sight. It brings our experiences under some order. It focuses them. Perhaps the same is true of the idea of 'order'. Maybe we need to invent the concept of order to make sense of the world. Perhaps there is no order in the world in just the same way that there is no cause in the world. If this is true, then the argument from design is completely overthrown.

But spare a thought for what this view of order means. It suggests that whatever the world was like we should invent neat classifications of our experience of it and so impose order upon the world from our own thoughts. There is a problem which springs from this view of such ideas as 'cause' and 'order'. *Why* do we need to think in these terms at all? For it seems that most people, down the ages, have shared this way of looking at the world, and even if different men have used different 'causes' and invented alternative 'orders' yet the concepts of order and cause have remained. Later we shall try to pay some attention to this difficult question.

The Problem of Evil

Close on the heels of the argument from design is the view that there must be a god in order to account for the goodness which we see in the world. In a sense this is to put the argument the other way round. More frequently the *lack* of any evidence of lasting good in the world has been used as an argument against the existence of God. If the presence of good in the world does not lead us to believe in a good God, does the presence of evil lead us to think that either God is an evil being or, more simply, that there is no God?

This is made more difficult by the problem of what we mean by 'good'. It may be that 'good' has the same kind of meaning as 'cause' and 'order' or that we use it to mean in the same way as we use 'cause' and 'order'. If this is true, and 'good' is a word we use to describe pleasant experiences, then we had better be careful not to make the mistake of seeking in the world what is invented in our minds. For perhaps the *world just is*; and the ideas of good and evil are our own concoctions.

Even if this is true, what we cannot doubt is that people all over the world suffer illness and pain. This is not an idea which helps us to understand the world. Pain is not our invention. It is a fact of human experience and its existence cannot easily be doubted. Who is prepared to say he has never experienced pain? So the argument about God and goodness turns into one about pain and suffering. Believers argue that God is all-powerful and completely good. Unbelievers ask why such a perfect being allows awful suffering in the world. They argue like this: 'If God cannot stop suffering then he is not all powerful; if he can but will not then he is not all good'. How is the believer able to answer such criticisms of his view?

First it is suggested that some small pain is necessary in order that people may enjoy greater good. For instance, we may suffer through getting wet in the rain, but the water we gain from the wet weather provides us with our food which is necessary for life. So the believer argues that some discomfort and pain must be suffered in order that we may enjoy much greater benefits.

There are straightforward replies to this view. To begin with, not all pains are so obviously for our eventual benefit as the discomfort of getting wet in the rain which provides our food. There are the pains which men suffer in earthquakes, volcanic eruptions, electrical storms and floods. It is hard to see what is the benefit of these violent events.

Also, surely an all powerful God could have created a world in which no pains at all were necessary—not even those which lead to a greater good. If he could not have created such a world, then it is argued, he cannot be all powerful. Believers sometimes argue against the first of these two objections that we do not know what further good might yet come out of earthquakes and storms etc so we are in no position to use their occurrence as an argument against God. And to the second objection believers may reply that God cannot do what is a contradiction; he cannot perform the logically impossible action. For instance, he cannot make something which is completely iron and at the same time is completely wood. That would be ridiculous. So they argue that God has done everything possible; he has made the best of all *possible* worlds.

Neither of these two replies satisfies the unbeliever. The first, about eventual good coming from earthquakes and storms seems too fanciful to be true. After all we have waited a long time for such good results to appear. And the second reply appears to limit the power of God in some way. For what else can it mean to say that God cannot do the impossible except that someone or something other than God decides what is possible and what is impossible in the first place? So both replies seem to fall down because in one way or another they limit the power of God. And in the beginning the believer defined God as an *all powerful* being. But is there anything wrong with the idea of a God who is not all powerful? A god who is very powerful but yet not almighty? Well such a being may exist, but it is misleading to call such a being 'God'. Someone who is not all powerful, who is limited by other factors, is more like man than God. He is a creature rather than a creator. And the believer would not worship such a subordinate or 'second rate' god. 'Worship' and 'reverence' are very important words to remember when talking of God. Besides, such a limited god is unsatisfactory for the unbeliever as well as for the believer. A creator who is limited by events and categories which he himself has not invented is no god. He is more like an assistant creator, a supporting cause in the existence of the world. In either case the idea of 'god' now considered is not that we started out with, not that of an almighty and perfectly good being.

The Argument based on Religious Experience

When people say that they feel something in their bones, they mean that they believe something beyond any doubt. The bones are too close to be doubted. So some argue that they 'know' God exists because they feel sure of him in just this way. How do they arrive at this belief? What happens in spite of all the contrary appearances and arguments to convince men of God's existence so certainly that they express their belief in the words 'I feel it in my bones'?

Let us be clear. This kind of belief is very personal. It gains its strength not from arguments of the mind but, usually, from deep emotional experience. This experience is often something very definite in the life of a person. So one might say, 'I know God exists because when my mother was very ill I prayed to him to spare her life and it seemed as though a soft warm light glowed in her room and she lived'. Not all religious experiences are as intense or as colourful as this, but this is the kind of event which frequently is alleged to have caused a person to accept the existence of God as a vital fact.

What are we to say about such experiences? Surely here is proof, personal and individual proof of God's existence? It is one thing to doubt, challenge and even disprove an intellectual argument which is being used to persuade one of God's existence. It is quite a different thing to doubt what appears to be personal proof or at least direct evidence of the existence of a good God. There seems to be something much more real, more definite and solid about the kind of experience mentioned here than any intellectual argument, however reasonable.

I think that personal religious experience is the best argument for the existence of God. But I don't think that even this argument is above criticism. There are many possible objections. First, how do I know that the experience of God's presence, to which I attach so much significance, was a real experience and not merely an hallucination, a vision or a dream? It is well known that we sometimes 'see' things which are not really there at all. And if we do this under normal conditions involving ordinary everyday objects, how much more likely it is that our senses should deceive us when we are tired, worried and anxious. It is often the case that religious experience, so called, occurs at these times—when we are in deep trouble or surrounded by great suffering. So surely such experiences may be misleading if they cause us to believe that they are the work of an almighty God.

Secondly, it is objected to the argument from religious experience that we bring these visions, strange or false perceptions—hallucinations upon ourselves at such times of stress because we hope against hope that something dramatic will happen to free us from our problem and our anxiety. So really what we later come to take as proof of the existence of God was no more than wishful thinking on our part at a moment of great distress.

Thirdly, even if we grant that these kinds of experience are caused by something or someone other than ourselves it does not follow that God is the cause. It may be that there is some mysterious power, about which we know next to nothing at the moment, which is unleashed at times of great emotion and stress. Although we know little of this force now, it is possible that in years to come it will be no more strange than electricity. Also, it is not unlikely that on occasions of great tension, such as occur during periods of serious illness, that human beings themselves, powered by great sympathy and feeling might generate a 'power' or a 'force' which can be experienced. Perhaps this is just an extreme version of feelings we can already describe as 'team spirit' or 'party atmosphere'.

Some believers might argue that this last objection is based on an idea more fanciful and unlikely than the existence of God: that it is less complicated to believe in God than in these mysterious forces. But we may reply that after all God, if he exists, is himself a kind of mysterious force. Besides we are more likely to have eventual success if we at least try to define odd experiences in the language of science than in mysterious words associated with God. If anyone doubts our action here, we need only point to the successful way in which science has, even in our own century, made clear many events and occurrences which were once thought to be mysterious.

Summary

We have looked at many different arguments for the existence of God and we have seen that there is no proof that there is such a being. But, before we all make up our minds to become atheists it is worth remembering that proof is something very difficult to achieve in philosophy and argument. We have met problems about proof in many other branches of our subject. But because, in one sense, we have been able to find no proof that the world we can see and touch really exists, we have not begun to live our lives as if there were no roads, cars, telephones or schools etc.... So we do not need to abandon a belief in God, if we already have such a belief, just because we cannot find an argument which proves that he exists. It is just as hard to prove that many other things of which we are even surer do actually exist. But we must remember not to try and argue for God or for anything else by using an argument we know to be inconclusive or fallacious. That is the point of philosophy and argument. We must be honest with ourselves as with those whom we are trying to convince by our reasoning. In an earlier section we saw the danger of arguing that because one argument was not correct therefore a particular thing did not exist. Remember the point of that chapter: just because St Thomas Aquinas' arguments are not proofs of God's existence does not, in itself, prove that there is no God. All it shows is that those particular arguments are not proofs.

But do all our arguments about God's existence amount to nothing? Is there anything to be said further about them? Is it possible that after all they may teach us something? Of course, a false argument leads nowhere in itself, but is it possible that many arguments, even if they are inconclusive, might help us form our opinions about the matter with which they deal?

First let us be sure to notice the difference between an argument which is false and one which is merely inconclusive. A false argument is more often than not a mistaken method of tackling a problem. So we should discover where the fallacy or mistake lies and then avoid the conclusions of that argument in the future. But an inconclusive argument is not necessarily a false one. It is simply an argument which, though not containing any errors, does not have in it enough relevant detail, properly set down, about the *conclusion* to which it tries to lead. I am not wanting to suggest that inconclusive arguments are all right, nor that many inconclusive arguments put together make a conclusive one. I am simply stating that we cannot discard incomplete arguments and cases as if they were false.

It may be that there is no conclusive argument for the existence of God for the very simple and straightforward reason that there is no God. But we are not bound to accept that this reason is the only one possible. It may be that there is a God, but as in many other areas of reasoning, we find difficulty in proving the fact. It is equally possible that there is no God. But we may reasonably ask whether all the inconclusive arguments do not, in the end, provide us at least with strong hints that there is a God.

Take, for example, the argument from religious experience (the feeling in the bones). It would not be accurate to call this argument false. It is rather incomplete, inconclusive. It does not prove that there is a God. But let us not confuse *proof* with *evidence*. The argument from religious experience might be said to give us some evidence about the problem of whether God exists or not. In other words, those arguments about God which are not downright fallacious and mistaken, might give us some *hints*, something upon which to base an investigation.

Some have said that the very fact that men seek God is proof that he exists. They have based this argument on what they take to be similar appetites and satisfactions in human life. For instance, we are hungry, there is food; we are thirsty, there is drink. It is argued that we can infer the existence of God in this way from our desire to believe in him. I do not accept this argument for two reasons.

First, some people are hungry and yet they do not find food. They starve. Others die of thirst. So we cannot say that the comparisons between these arguments and a similar one for the existence of God are exact in their picture of what the world is like. Unfulfilled appetites do exist. In the same way belief in God or need for God does not mean that God exists.

Secondly, it is not true that all men desire that God should exist. So the comparison between desire for food and desire for God is not an exact one. All men have an appetite for food; not all are so earnest in their wish that there should be a God.

But while I cannot agree that belief in God is in itself a proof that there is a God, I think that the fact that most or at least many men and women have believed in God, is a piece of evidence in favour of God's existence. It is a hint. Having said this I must guard against being misunderstood. Hints may be discarded and discounted. So this particular evidence is inconclusive; it may amount to nothing. It is simply that I find the common fact of belief fascinating; I regard it as something to be kept in mind when trying to decide whether or not there is a God.

In the same way it is possible and even sensible to regard with respect all those personal hints about God which other people tell us out of their religious experience. It may be that they are wrong and misguided, even deluded. But if this kind of experience is not allowed to count as *evidence* for the existence of God, then it is difficult to see what could *possibly* count as evidence. Remember that by 'evidence' I mean only something worth consideration, something to be kept in mind and thought about, measured, weighed and evaluated in connection with a particular problem. It may be that in the end the evidence is not strong enough.

So I believe that the old arguments for the existence of God have value in that they remind us that this problem is one which has concerned many men down the centuries. And because this question has been asked by every generation of men, I believe it to be an important one. Perhaps one generation will answer the question, and the matter will be settled one way or the other. I don't know, though I doubt it. I doubt whether any of the problems of philosophy will ever be finally solved. It seems that every 'solution' throws up more problems. Though I do believe that the fact that men keep trying to answer these problems tells us a lot about men. On the following pages, after the usual exercise, are a few questions about the purpose of philosophy. This book will possess a measure of usefulness if you are encouraged by it to consider the value of thinking philosophically.

Exercise
(1) *Make a list of some of the ways in which people use the word 'God'.*
(2) *Is it really possible to imagine that the world began by accident?*
(3) *'Everything in the world has its cause, so the world must have a cause'. Talk about this.*
(4) *Is it reasonable to believe that all the order and sequence which we sense in the universe really is just a lucky accident?*
(5) *Give ten examples of design in the universe. Do these convince you of God's existence?*
(6) *What might be the difference between God and a designer of the universe?*
(7) *What difficulties are there in the argument from design?*
(8) *How do we decide what is 'order' and what is 'disorder'?*
(9) *'If God is almighty, he would not allow wars'. How might a believer argue against this?*
(10) *Is this the best of all possible worlds?*
(11) *'If God existed he would have shown us a good use for the desert'. Would he?*
(12) *'I know God exists because he answers my prayers'. What can be argued against this?*
(13) *Are feelings of joy, hope, love, fear etc . . . arguments for God's existence?*
(14) *What kind of experience might what is called 'religious experience' really be?*
(15) *Can an inconclusive argument be a hint?*
(16) *Does the fact that many have believed in God make you believe in him? If so, why? If not, why not?*

The Purpose of Philosophy
(1) *What is the difference between evidence and proof?*
(2) *Name some of the problems of philosophy.*
(3) *What is particularly philosophical about philosophical questions?*
(4) *Will any particular problems of philosophy ever be solved? If so, which ones? Can you solve any such problem? If so, how? If not, why not?*
(5) *What is the point in trying to think philosophically?*

Further Reading

(1) GOOD ELEMENTARY INTRODUCTIONS TO PHILOSOPHY
Learning to Philosophise, E. R. Emmet (Penguin)
An Introduction to Philosophical Analysis, J. Hospers (Routledge & Kegan Paul)
The Problems of Philosophy, B. Russell (OUP paperback)

(2) A RATHER MORE SUBSTANTIAL AND EXCELLENT SUMMARY
A Hundred Years of Philosophy, J. Passmore (Pelican)

(3) FAMOUS TWENTIETH CENTURY BOOKS ON PHILOSOPHY
The Problem of Knowledge, A. J. Ayer (Pelican)
The Concept of Mind, G. Ryle (Peregrine)
Sense and Sensibilia, J. L. Austin (OUP paperback)
The Meaning of Meaning, C. K. Ogden & I. A. Richards (Routledge & Kegan Paul)
Logic and Language, (First and Second Series), Ed A. G. N. Flew (Blackwell)
An Inquiry into Meaning and Trust, B. Russell (Pelican)
The Theory of Meaning, Ed G. H. R. Parkinson (OUP paperback)
Definition, R. Robinson (OUP)
Dilemmas, G. Ryle (Cambridge)
Philosophical Investigations, L. Wittgenstein: translated by G. E. M. Anscombe (Blackwell)

(4) MORAL PHILOSOPHY
Ethics Since 1900, Mary Warnock (OUP paperback)
The Language of Morals, R. M. Hare (OUP paperback)
Freedom and Reason, R. M. Hare (OUP paperback)
Ethics, G. E. Moore (OUP paperback)
Ethics and Language, C. L. Stevenson (Yale)
An Examination of the Place of Reason in Ethics, S. E. Toulmin (Cambridge)

(5) PHILOSOPHY OF RELIGION
Introduction to Religious Philosophy, Geddes MacGregor (Macmillan)
New Essays in Philosophical Theology, Ed A. G. N. Flew and A. C. MCIntyre (SCM)
Historical Selections in the Philosophy of Religion, Ed N. Smart (SCM)

(6) CLASSICS OF PHILOSOPHY
Republic, Plato (Penguin Classics)

Metaphysics, Aristotle (Penguin Classics)
Meditations, R. Descartes (Penguin Classics)
Discourse on Method, R. Descartes (Penguin Classics)
An Essay Concerning the Human Knowledge, Berkeley (Fontana)
Enquiries Concerning the Human Understanding and Concerning the Principles of Morals, D. Hume (Oxford)
Critique of Pure Reason, I. Kant, translated by Kemp-Smith (New York St Martins)
Utilitarianism, J. S. Mill (Fontana)

Many of these works in sections 3, 4, 5 and 6 are difficult, and the student who wishes to improve his knowledge of philosophy is strongly recommended to read one or more of the introductions in section 1 and then John Passmore's book before looking into the more advanced volumes.